Praise for *Tiny Vo*

Toria talks about being 'that teacher' and reading through these pages, one realises 'that teacher' has a multitude of guises, quirks and styles, but a commonality of belief to put children and colleagues first. Here is a whole year's worth of staff-meeting reading with pieces short but detailed enough to generate debate around the role of the SENCO, the 'why' in EYFS, mentoring, challenging issues around diversity and how we can all grow as leaders. There are stories to cause the reader to reflect, to laugh, to cry and to realise what they have been saying for years has been right all along.

Andrew Cowley, author of *The Wellbeing Toolkit*
and *The Wellbeing Curriculum*

I absolutely loved this book. The teacher voice that shines through every story is one of dedication, compassion, gentle self-deprecating humour and authenticity. Tired of the predictable positioning of so-called 'edu-celebrities', this group of colleagues write honestly and they write from the heart. Our profession is full of teachers who care and who have so much wisdom to offer. I am so proud to be a teacher; reading this book made my heart sing. Thank you to everyone who reads this and allows their tiny voice to become a little louder. I applaud you.

Dame Alison Peacock, Chief Executive,
Chartered College of Teaching

Tiny Voices Talk is as much about kindness as it is about education. I suspect that many of the teachers in the book would agree that the main aim of education is to develop kindness – towards others and ourselves. We work in a profession where the job is never finished and is often unsatisfactory. We have to be sufficiently resilient to care for ourselves, our colleagues and the children. I found the experience of reading the book rather like opening up a little treasure box, packed with intriguing stories of teachers' lives and what they have learned. There are gems to be found in sharing the reality of our professional lives.

Dr Pie Corbett, writer, educational consultant
and leader of Talk for Writing

Professionals from across the educational sector have contributed towards this compelling book, empowering others to use their voices – their passion being the golden thread running throughout.

Anoara Mughal, teacher and author of *Think! Metacognition-Powered Primary Teaching*

There is nothing tiny about this book, which provides a platform for educators with 'quieter voices' – those we would not usually know about. We all have educational experiences and insights to share, given half a chance. And there are powerful points within this book that deserve to be shared with a wider audience. Bravo, Toria, for making this possible.

Bukky Yusuf, Senior Leader, leadership coach and co-editor of *The Big Book of Whole School Wellbeing*

The #TinyVoiceTalks concept is about connecting, engaging and empowering educators. *Tiny Voices Talk* is full of wisdom and practical support that informs and challenges thinking. Whether you are starting your teaching journey, leading a large setting or have decades of experience, this book should be part of every school's professional development library. With topics ranging from transition to schemata, this is a book I will revisit again and again. Toria Bono has expertly curated a diverse and informed range of voices and I highly recommend this book.

Simon Kidwell, School Principal and Vice President of the NAHT School Leaders' Union

Bono has created inspiring, readable and relatable chapters – the voices are diverse and the messages run deep. Each pacey, quick read digs into an aspect of education which encourages you, the reader, to question, empathise and reflect.

Chris Dyson, Head Teacher, Parklands Primary School, National Leader of Education

Lots of tiny voices can often make a powerful collective roar. In this book, Toria Bono does just that. The opinion, expertise, experience and insight of committed professionals come together from all corners of education. The tiny voices that are often not heard are both compelling and authoritative.

David Whitaker, Director of Learning,
Wellspring Academy Trust

If you are looking for a book that will inspire and motivate you and one that you can't put down, this book is for you; it will grab you from the first to the last page.

John Magee, author of *Kindness Matters*, founder of
Kindness Matters Educational Online Courses

Tiny Voices Talk: how this is needed in the current educational landscape. Education discourse played out on social media and in books is dominated by behemoth voices often detached from the realities and joys of the classroom. The lethal mutations of once prescient, powerful pedagogies and practices have been debased and reduced to tribute band status, repeated ad infinitum in talks, books and magazines. Toria Bono and her quiet army of tiny voices have begun to redress the balance in this seminal book. Each contributor speaks with authenticity about the power of the tiny voice and the joy of teaching. The book is divided into sections covering topics that are universally applicable to any teacher in any classroom. The empathy engendered by the tiny voices stirs the reader, takes them on a journey of discovery of the real voices of teachers and brings to the fore issues hitherto hidden in plain sight. There are also real and actionable tips and advice for teachers at whatever stage of their journey. This book will inspire, invigorate and identify the tiny voice in all who read it.

Phil Naylor, author of *Naylor's Natter*

This is a brilliant set of anecdotes and advice from such a range of people and places that you won't fail to recognise yourself in some of the chapters or gain some new knowledge or information that will help you in your role, whatever that may be! What's so good about this is that these aren't all 'superstar' or 'celebrity' voices either – they're tiny voices that have been brave enough to speak to Toria to tell their tale and to show, in doing so, that you could do the same! It's inspirational.

Rich Simpson, founder of #kindnessripple
on Twitter, Teacher Hug Radio presenter,
book reviewer for whatiread.co.uk

I 'met' Toria at the start of the pandemic as part of a virtual network of like-minded educators who became firm friends. It was obvious from the start that we shared the same values, dedication to education and passion for equality. Moreover, we are both committed in empowering educators to use and share their knowledge with others so that all our children are served well. Every voice matters, even if it starts out tiny. This book should be on an essential reading list for anyone who is trying to find their feet in, and out of, the classroom. A treasure trove of wisdom from a myriad of voices in education, every single contribution has at least one thing that you can take away to ponder, reflect, use and share with others.

Sharifah Lee, Head Teacher, Dorney School

TINY **VOICES** TALK

EDUCATION, ENGAGEMENT, EMPOWERMENT

TORIA BONO
TINY **VOICE** TALKS

ındependent
thinking press

First published by
Independent Thinking Press
Crown Buildings, Bancyfelin, Carmarthen, Wales, SA33 5ND, UK
www.independentthinkingpress.com
and
Independent Thinking Press
PO Box 2223, Williston, VT 05495, USA
www.crownhousepublishing.com
Independent Thinking Press is an imprint of Crown House Publishing Ltd.

First published 2022.

Tiny Voice Talks logo © 2022 Tiny Voice Talks.

Edited by Ian Gilbert.

British Library Cataloguing-in-Publication Data
A catalogue entry for this book is available from the British Library.
Print ISBN 978-178135411-7
Mobi ISBN 978-178135415-5
ePub ISBN 978-178135416-2
ePDF ISBN 978-178135417-9

LCCN 2022936629
Printed and bound in the UK by
CPi Antony Rowe, Chippenham, Wiltshire

This book is dedicated:

- To the memory of my father, Thomas George Miskelly. He always wanted the best for me and, while he was never enamoured with me going into teaching, I am pretty sure he would have loved to read a book with my name on the front.

- To the person I would have loved to teach me – my mum. I remember watching her teach and hoping that one day I could be just like her in the classroom. She inspired me more than she will ever know.

In life, finding a voice is speaking and living the truth. Each of you is an original. Each of you has a distinctive voice. When you find it, your story will be told. You will be heard.

John Grisham

Tiny Voices Foreword

We live in a loud world. Make a fuss. Make some noise. Make a scene. Be heard. Be loud. Get followed. Give a monkey a megaphone and it becomes the loudest animal in the jungle. It doesn't make it the smartest though. Build a following, be controversial and turn online bullying into a spectator sport – that's the way to make people listen. You'll get a book deal out of it too, if you're quick.

Loud is good. Louder is better. Want to be heard? Speak up. What's wrong with you?

Of course, as with everything in the beautiful world of education, there is always another way. And Toria Bono's Tiny Voices platform is one such way.

Quietly, carefully, without a fuss, she has created an online space where people – lovely, caring people who also happen to be wonderful educators – can meet, talk and share. Through her Twitter community – #TinyVoiceTalks – she has made it possible for over 30,000 educators to have their voices heard. Quiet voices. Tiny voices. Voices with something to say, not shout.

I had the pleasure of being interviewed by Toria during the second lockdown, for Teacher Hug Radio. We talked education, childhood, grief, well-being, bird watching with your ears in magical woodlands. She has her own *Tiny Voice Talks* podcast too. Many of the contributors to this book have had the pleasure of being interviewed by her. Follow the QR code link on the following page or visit tinyvoicetalks.com to have a listen. In these podcasts, she has also interviewed many 'names' from the world of education. But even big voices use their 'inside voice' when they are talking to Toria.

From a fabulous hashtag and an ongoing series of podcasts that never cease to inspire and inform, we now have this book. Tiny voices talking through the page. Surprising voices and helpful ones. Informative voices and supportive ones. Voices that sound like yours. Voices that sound nothing like it. Voices that make you laugh. Voices that move you. Voices that sometimes rise up in a challenge, but never a shout.

Once you have found a quiet moment to read this book, I then recommend you take time to listen. There are tiny voices all around you. In our loud world, they are easy to miss. You might be in the staffroom. Or in a classroom. You might be in an assembly or among parents. You might be in a large meeting. You might be in a small one. When you stop listening just to the loud ones, you hear what the tiny ones have to say. You'll be amazed.

You might even hear your own tiny voice in that way too.

Ian Gilbert, founder, Independent Thinking,
Rotterdam

Acknowledgements

This book would have been in no way possible without certain people's belief in my tiny voice. Thank you, firstly, to everyone who shows up every Tuesday on the #TinyVoiceTalks thread on Twitter. You were there when I felt unheard. Together we have found our voices and continue to grow. Thank you to all my podcast guests – thank you for trusting that I will help you to find your voice and be heard by others. Thank you also to those of you who listen and support the quieter voices in education – it means a lot.

I want to thank all of those voices who sent in their submissions for this book in July 2021. Some of them lie among the pages of this book, but others couldn't be included this time as I was inundated with submissions. In truth, I never expected so many and am grateful to everyone who put finger to keyboard.

I don't think there would be a book without Ian Gilbert. He appears in so many authors' acknowledgements because he is truly fabulous. He believed in my ability to create the *Tiny Voices Talk* book long before I did. He patiently talked me through the process and was there each time I had a crisis of confidence (and there were a few times). He knew what I wanted to create and respected my opinions, and understood that preserving the unique voice of each contributor was so important to me; for that, I will be forever grateful. Thank you, Ian.

Thank you to all the amazing people at Crown House who, alongside Ian, guided me through creating a book from all the submissions. This wasn't as easy as I thought it would be (I have always been a tad naive), but with their help I have found my way.

Finally, I want to acknowledge the love and support of my family. Without my sister Caroline's input, I would never have been a teacher. She was the person who suggested it initially, and I will be forever grateful to her for setting me off on this journey. My husband, Delmar, is never surprised when I start a new project and always quietly cheers me on from the sidelines. He listens when I tell him that I am worried I have taken on a little too much and reassures me that everything will be fine – he's always right. My daughter Claudia is also never surprised when I start something new and she has feigned interest from time to time when I have talked to her about the book – I have hugely appreciated this. My mum and step-dad, Simon, stopped being surprised with my endeavours a very long time ago and have also been wonderfully supportive. They have read many a version of this book and my mum's feedback (as a retired teacher) has been invaluable. I truly don't know what I would do without any of them. Thank you, family!

Contents

Introduction

Toria Bono

Possunt quia posse videntur
(They can because they think they can)

Virgil

Have you ever heard of the butterfly effect? The idea was conceived over 45 years ago by Edward Lorenz, a meteorology professor, who wanted to demonstrate that small, insignificant events can lead to much larger significant events over time. Lorenz proposed that the simple act of a butterfly flapping its wings in Tokyo could lead to a tornado in Tennessee. He didn't mean it quite as literally as some have taken it, but the idea is nonetheless a powerful one. The simple act of a butterfly flapping its wings could lead to a small change that eventually could create a significant event. Butterflies, therefore, have more power than at first supposed. All they need to do is start flapping their wings!

Related, in a tenable way, is my fascination with creatures that fly. When I was growing up, my dad had a picture in his office. The picture was of two seagulls and it said 'They can because they think they can.' That picture fascinated me but it wasn't until much later that the quote (from Virgil) made much sense to me. Birds, like butterflies, don't wonder if they can fly. They don't sit on a branch, cogitating about whether they are going to successfully fly or, indeed, look as good as their peers in doing so; they just do it.

How many times have you sat in a meeting with a good idea developing inside your mind? How many times have you considered sharing the idea but found yourself silent instead? If you are like me, it will be many, many times. I have wanted to share my ideas but have found myself overthinking about how others would respond and ultimately have decided that the best thing to do is remain silent.

This happened on Twitter too when I started my journey on there in January 2020. Every word that I considered tweeting I deleted, for fear of failure or judgement. I wanted to join in, but was scared that my 280 characters would be the wrong ones. In February 2020, I started #TinyVoiceTuesdayUnites on Twitter (now #TinyVoiceTalks) as a way for the quieter voices in education to have their say. I flapped my wings and others joined in. The #TinyVoiceTalks community continues to meet on Twitter every Tuesday and it is wonderful to see people finding their voice and the courage to be heard. What is even more wonderful is the power of the community that is listening.

That community led me to start the *Tiny Voice Talks* podcast in August 2020. The podcast is devoted to hearing the quieter voices – giving them a platform and letting them know that their voice matters. What I discovered, as I spoke to more and more people from the world of education, is that so many of us have things that we want to say but are fearful of expressing for a myriad of reasons. Instead, we just keep quiet and nod agreeably with the bigger voices – even when we disagree. What became clear to me, though, was that when tiny voices talk, three amazing things happen:

1. They share surprising insights and ideas.

2. They realise they are not so tiny.

3. They empower other tiny voices to talk too.

I think the Tiny Voice Talks effect is very similar to the butterfly effect. When we find our voices and use them, even if we are only whispering, change happens. I have received so many messages from people who have spoken up and instigated change in their classroom, school and professional lives. Spurred on by Tiny Voice Talks, they found their voices and started using them.

The power of our voice is incredible and that is why we now have this book. When I asked for submissions, I wrote this:

> This book is going to be a great resource full of practical ideas and little wins from tiny voices across the educational spectrum. Where tiny voices talk to tiny voices. Although we will have many tiny voices covering many different topics, the *Golden Thread* that holds it all together – and what will make this book truly special – is what it also reveals about the power we have when we find our voice and use it.

And that is what you have – a great resource, full of practical ideas and little wins; my hope is that it will help you to find your voice too. I have given you space for your voice at the end of the book. For those of you just finding your voice, here are my top tips – write down things that resonate with you, consider why they do so and then think if you need to make changes because of this. It may be that you want to make changes to your approach to teaching and learning. It may be that you want to make changes to your leadership style or it may be that you want to make changes to your life. Whatever it is, write it down and then (and this is important) start flapping your wings and finding your voice. Voice what you are thinking and change will happen. If you doubt yourself, remember that birds never wonder if they can fly; they just do.

Part I

Tiny Voices Talk About Being That Teacher

At the tender age of 12, I was in an art lesson and my work was held up. Now, I wasn't a confident artist and I was so proud that the teacher had chosen to show my piece to the class. I sat there filled with a mix of anxiety and excitement. 'This is what not to do,' she said. I was crushed.

Not all my teachers were like this. I was lucky enough, on occasions, to have 'that teacher'. You know the one. The one who saw you and who heard you. The one who really understood you.

When I was 8, I was taught by Mrs S. She knew that I was a chatterbox (not a lot changes there) but she also knew that I wanted to try hard and do my best. In her class, for the first time in my school life, I felt seen, heard and understood.

When I was 10, we moved to California for a brief period and I went to school in Santa Monica. This all sounds very glamorous, but it wasn't really. I was away from my friends, my school and everything familiar. My fourth-grade teacher was Mrs D and she believed in me. This completely changed my experience. By the time I left that school, I was confident and happy to be me.

Then, back in the UK and doing my GCSEs, I went to the chemistry teacher and asked for some extra support. 'Frankly Victoria,' she replied, 'you are beyond help.'

This memory, alongside many others I could share with you, erased my confidence. By the time I finished school, I ended up with very little self-belief. I had learned by then that teachers can help children stand tall or crush them to the ground.

I wish I could tell you about more teachers who touched my life in a positive way, but I can't. To most of the teachers who taught me, I was invisible. I tried hard but I was a B-grade student. I behaved well (once I learned to stop chatting) so I went unnoticed. I was beige. I needed teachers like Mrs S and Mrs D who made me feel all the colours of the rainbow, not teachers who were content with me being beige.

Are you 'that teacher', like Mrs S and Mrs D? I really hope that I am. In my classroom I have a sign by my desk and it says 'Believe'. I keep it there to remind the children that I believe in them. And that they should believe in themselves too.

The chapters in this section are devoted to being 'that teacher' and the difference we can make when we are. At the end, take time to find your voice and write down what you do for the young people in your care. I know you care because you are reading this book. How do they know you do?

Chapter 1
Be That Teacher

Leanne Herring

Be that teacher: the one who is not afraid to veer from the plan; the one who gets excited to be directing an end-of-term show; the one whose enthusiasm gets the eye rolls in the staffroom. Be the teacher who discovers an old rusty key on the pavement and pounces on it to use as writing inspiration later. The teacher who dresses up in whatever it takes to get the class talking about the best flavour of ice cream – and knows how to stop them talking too.

Be the teacher who questions the things that don't make sense, who asks for the reasons behind a new incentive, who points out – when faced with yet another (purchased) scheme of work – that anyone can read from a script, but a teacher inspires beyond a text. Be the one who goes above and beyond to learn the skills to reach those children who may feel lost or overwhelmed in a bustling classroom, who brings into line the disruptive children seeking the attention they might not receive anywhere else, and who shows how far a love of learning can take us all. The one who sings, dances and performs, telling stories that make children laugh and jokes that don't; who runs around the playground in the rain – take that 'wet playtime'!

Children do not need another carbon copy of a previous teacher, delivering lessons that anyone could deliver. They need role models who encourage creativity and change and who express individuality.

Being that teacher is hard. At times during your career, it will feel like all you can do is jump through the right hoops at the right time, fall in line with the tick-box clip-chart culture and nod along to the things that most dishearten you. But within the walls of your classroom, you're the boss and those hoops can be whatever size and shape you need them to be to match the needs of those who matter most to a teacher.

Never be afraid to venture (back) into a child's world and embrace imagination and fun. What other job is there where you get paid to build a den, skip across a playground or make cakes out of mud? And how much more engaging is that than asking 30 inert children to turn to page 23 of a textbook with a forgettable title? Think about your own memories of school. Everyone remembers their favourite worksheet? I don't think so. We do remember that time Mrs Strong threw caution to the wind, the unexpected happened and we became truly excited not only about learning but about ourselves.

Never underestimate the power you have as a teacher, armed with your special weapons of awe and wonder. Always remember how you can build confidence in a wary child that no generic curriculum can ever do. Data, bar charts and statistics have their place, but they are not what counts. They just guide us to do what counts. Creating moments that matter is what being a great teacher is all about. And teachers who create those moments live forever.

Be that teacher.

Leanne Herring is a primary school teacher and writer based in Essex who has been teaching in the early years foundation stage and Key Stage 1 for the last 10 years. She has completed a master's in psycholinguistics and now works as an educational content creator specialising in phonics.

Chapter 2

Self-Esteem Is (Still) the Key to Learning

Dr Clare Campbell

In my very first essay as a primary teaching student over 22 years ago, I wrote 'Self-esteem is the key to learning.' I believed it then but I know it now.

Self-esteem is perhaps best defined as feeling both capable and lovable, and a child with low self-esteem is not in a good place to learn. How could they be? Learning involves having the courage to be open to new possibilities and take risks on the way. It exposes you. If you feel you are going to fail and people will like you even less when you do, you are not going to want to put yourself on the line to even try.

This is why it is vital that so much of an educator's job is about developing great relationships with their pupils, backed up by the quality of the pastoral care they give them. After all, children's mental health and well-being is paramount – even more so during a pandemic that has taken its emotional toll on us all.

Your job, then, is to do everything in your power to build up a child's self-esteem each day. And keep at it day after day. After all, self-esteem can be a very fragile as well as a fluttering thing. It can appear in one part of the curriculum only to disappear in another. The child who feels 10 feet tall in drama may feel tiny in a numeracy lesson.

That is why I love the creative subjects so much. Art, dance, drama, music, poetry and creative writing are areas of the curriculum where there are no wrong answers. Through the creative arts, children can express themselves without the fear of getting it 'wrong'.

In my school we use art therapy for the children who need additional support and we employ an art psychotherapist part time to work with our children. Art therapy is all about making art while building positive relationships with the therapist as you do. The end product is not important. What counts is the process the children go through to get there: one they enjoy and through which they can really express themselves in a way they have been unable to with the written or spoken word.

Often our children discover an otherwise hidden natural talent in art and go on to pursue it as a hobby – something which gives them great joy and a sense of peace and mindfulness, and helps raise their self-esteem. When you are good at something, you see yourself developing new skills and unlocking your creative potential. It feels good. You feel good. And all children are good at something. As teachers, our job is to find out what that is rather than spending all our time focusing on what they can't do.[1]

Linked to that, I think one of the most damaging things we can do for a child's self-esteem is to underestimate them. To have low expectations of them and impose a ceiling on their natural gifts and talents is the opposite of what teaching should be about. That is why, in my school, we are not driven by the data. Children are so much more than a SAT score, a phonics screening test outcome or a GCSE result.

Remember too that the education system sets one child against another. It's all about the achievements of the individual, not the group. For some children to do well, we need others to do less well. Yet, we have all seen the outcome when children work creatively *together* to produce incredible things.

During the early stages of the pandemic, our head girl, Emily, was diagnosed with leukaemia at the age of 11. What followed was a punishing schedule of chemotherapy, yet she was still attending online lessons from her hospital bed and completing schoolwork to her usual high standards.

Even though the lockdown rules meant we were all at our most alone, this little girl and her family brought our community together. We focused

---

1   Something to bear in mind at parent consultation events.

on a range of whole-school projects that could be completed in school bubbles, or at home by our 'stay-at-home heroes', and we made lockdown love hearts which they decorated beautifully for Emily, with messages and prayers for her recovery. We also made butterflies of kindness which we sent to her hospital ward to cheer her up. For those children who needed them, we sent art materials home, and we also sent supplies to Emily's ward so that her new friends who were also having cancer treatment could join in too. Children and families even sent in jokes and we complied a huge joke book for her with the help of teachers on Twitter.

We also created beautiful artwork for her and then encouraged celebrities from all over the country to join in with a 'Thumbs up for Emily' campaign on social media. Stars from Emily's favourite soaps, *Hollyoaks*, *Emmerdale* and *Coronation Street* became involved, as did the likes of Gary Lineker, Lord Alan Sugar, Craig Revel Horwood and Joe Wicks. She is a Salford Reds rugby fan and her favourite player, Jackson Hastings, wore special rugby boots dedicated to her in one match and then gave them to her in person afterwards. We also created a whole-school art exhibition dedicated to Emily in the hall. Working with a local artist, Emma Evans, we decorated the glass entrance to the school with rainbow love hearts, each one representing a prayer said for Emily by our school family.

But it wasn't all about helping Emily. Together we spread the support and positivity even further with Emily's classmates going on sponsored bike rides, shaving their heads, making and selling little bead angels and more. With the support of Emily's amazing family too, we raised over £4,500 for Royal Manchester Children's Hospital and Emily managed to buy every single toy on the children's ward wish list. Her legacy will live on in Ward 84.

It would have been easy to underestimate the resilience of a young girl who was diagnosed with a terrible illness. And that of her classmates. Yet Emily and the whole school did things that I never expected or dreamed they could do. But why wait to be faced with terrible adversity to discover what children are really capable of? We can all learn so much from our children about dignity, integrity, compassion and kindness. When we recognise this, and celebrate it each day, we can really make a positive difference to their self-esteem.

I am typing this after watching our Year 6 leavers' show, *The Greatest Show-man*. It was a truly wonderful event with all children taking part. Emily, back at school and healthy now, sang a solo in her starring role and, of course, there wasn't a dry eye in the house.

Left: Emily in Manchester Children's Hospital with posters from her classmates
Right: Butterflies for Emily from children at St Charles RC Primary School

Emily after chemotherapy for childhood cancer

Dr Clare Campbell has been a head teacher since 2009 and a teacher since 1999. She has lectured in education at the University of Manchester, Manchester Metropolitan University, Liverpool Hope and Tangaza University in Nairobi. She is the mother of two teenage boys. Her publications include A Year of Mindfulness, Drawn to the Word, Be the Change and What Is Beauty? She has written and illustrated children's books including The Q and Mousa the Homeless Mouse.

Chapter 3
Children Deserve Better Period Education

Gemma Clark

Period education is part of my job. I'm an upper-school primary teacher in Scotland and it's a part of that role I *really* enjoy. I get the feeling I may be in the minority though, and I would like to use my 'tiny voice' to put forward some suggestions, based on my experience, for making period education better.

First things first. However it may be approached in your school, period education is *not* sex education. Yet so often the former is turned into a subsection of the latter and, in doing so, falls foul of the strict policies that teachers must adhere to when talking about sex.

Not that long ago, Scotland became one of the first countries in the world to make period products available for free. We also enjoy a more progressive approach to period education that differs from what you perhaps received (or did not receive) when you were at school. That traditional and still widely practised approach will have involved you at around 10 years old finding yourself either included in or excluded from a special assembly, depending on your gender. The origins of this approach are shrouded in the mists of time but probably relate to a combination of a need-to-know mentality and an attempt to avoid any sense of embarrassment on the part of the girls (or the female PE teacher who ended up with the job of delivering the talk). Such an approach is problematic for three primary reasons:

- Firstly, boys should also understand how the human body works, even bodies different from their own. Othering girls is also not helpful for all sorts of reasons and an awareness of one's own body and what it might do of its own accord is a lesson boys need too, especially given the adult male's infamous reticence about getting help when it is needed.

- Secondly, age 10 can be too late for period education anyway, as some girls may have started their periods as young as 8.

- Finally, it can mean denying transgender children information they need. Schools have an obligation to be inclusive, regardless of the viewpoint of any individual staff member (or parent). On that topic, another throwback is that of sending letters home, prior to the period education lessons, advising parents of their right to remove their children from the session. While parents have rights, of course, children do too and 'access to information' is one of the articles of the UN Convention on the Rights of the Child.[1] Children have the right to understand what will happen to their own bodies during puberty.

Period education, in other words, should start younger, be for everyone and there should be no opt-out caveats. Otherwise, we perpetuate the stigma, shame and taboo that exists.

The revolutionary book *Period Power* by Masie Hill made me realise how little I knew about periods, even as a woman in my thirties.[2] As a result, I would argue there should be a whole unit of lessons on the topic, rather than a solitary lesson or special assembly. In this way, children will gain a more thorough understanding of the menstrual cycle, of how the interplay of hormones will affect them and, ultimately, of themselves.

One analogy Hill employs, and that I have found particularly useful, is likening the menstrual cycle to the seasons. In this model, the week of the period when you bleed is like winter and, just like in winter, you may feel more tired than usual and more in need of rest. The week after the period is spring, with your energy starting to return ready for the week of ovulation – summer – when energy levels are at their highest and the associated

---

1   See https://www.unicef.org/child-rights-convention/convention-text.
2   Maisie Hill, *Period Power: Harness Your Hormones and Get Your Cycle Working for You* (London: Green Tree Publishing, 2019).

hormones bestow that precious feel-good factor. Autumn appears, as it inevitably does, the week before the period begins. Now your energy and emotions begin to change again and there may be that dip in energy you associate with darker nights and knowing winter is just round the corner.

Using this simple analogy, children can then be easily taught how to track their cycles, using this knowledge to better organise their lives. For example, they can learn not only to plan ahead, using the higher energy phases of the cycle to their full advantage, but also to be prepared to take things easier around the 'winter time' of their cycle, learning to practise self-care and to rest where necessary.

Talking of rest, in a school system that seems to be all about what children are doing – and whether they are succeeding in what they are doing – understanding and promoting the many benefits of rest is in everyone's interests. I would argue that teachers can lead the way towards this cultural shift. Rest is a necessary yet apparently radical act in a culture obsessed with measurable productivity. As teachers, we can be our own worst enemies when it comes to overworking and not doing enough to profit from doing nothing. Talk to your children about the importance of downtime, screen-free time, sleep and simply resting: a message relevant for both boys and girls.

Rather than turning period education into some awkward secret, taking place behind closed hall curtains, it can and should be an empowering experience for all. There are cultures around the world who celebrate *menarche* (the first period) with ceremonies and special rituals. For example, some indigenous American communities celebrate it with a 'sunrise' festival where they wear special clothes, participate in sacred rituals and receive gifts. There is a tradition in Japan to celebrate a child's first period with a special family meal. There are also cultures who see menstruation as a sacred time, when the person receives wisdom.

Surely our children deserve such empowering and life-affirming moments too, not the awkwardness and stigma they currently inherit from often awkward and stigmatised adults. So, let's start having these conversations and let's make those changes today. Who knows? Maybe in a few years girls will be asking for *menarche* ceremonies in the same way many do for prom dresses.

Gemma Clark is a dyslexic psychology graduate and primary school teacher from Scotland. She is passionate about inclusive education and health and well-being. She is also a Massage in Schools instructor and children and family yoga instructor. She believes in taking a well-being-focused and holistic approach to teaching children.

Chapter 4

Every Teacher Needs a Champion

Emma Courtney

If you have been in education in the last 10 years, at some point you will have sat through *that* TED Talk. You know the one: 'Every kid needs a champion.' The one where American teacher, Rita Pierson, implores us to champion a kid. I bet every single word she utters resonated with you. I bet you can hear her now:

> Every child deserves a champion – an adult who will never give up on them, who understands the power of connections and insists that they become the best that they can possibly be.[1]

So that's exactly what you then do. You pick your kid, usually the one who puts you through your paces every single day. The one who colourfully tells you where to stick your cheery 'Good morning', who informs you that they are indeed 'present' by kicking the door on the way in, who never has breakfast, who never has money for tag/mufti/Children in Need day, whose parents you have never seen, who you have chased up the street in your heels more than once, the one whose corner you are forever fighting in the staffroom. Then the day comes when they leave. They may even replace their habitual four-letter profanity with a goodbye. But then again, they may not. Either way, they go. Every so often, you wonder how they are

---

1   Rita Pierson, Every kid needs a champion [video], *TED* (May 2013). Available at: https://www.ted.com/talks/rita_pierson_every_kid_needs_a_champion?language=en.

doing. You may even see them on the street. You share a secret smile when you see that they are wearing a uniform. Phew, they are still in school. Thank goodness for that.

Years pass like this. Every year you find that kid to champion, until that call comes (and it will come). The most exciting call you could possibly get. The call to be a head. Your tiny voice will finally be heard! Great! Make it as loud as you can. Make that difference. And let me tell you, it's everything you thought it would be. And more! But, you know what? It's also hard. Not in a 'dealing with difficult parents, taking the rap when the inspectors aren't happy, turning up at school because of a sewage emergency at 7 a.m. on a Sunday' hard. It's worse than that – you enter the waiting place.

In the waiting place, you sit behind your desk while Class 8 do the parachute experiment; you always loved that lesson, so it is hard. You are out of school for a meeting about a Portacabin while Class 12 read one of your favourite books – you hope the teacher does the voices properly. In the waiting place, a nagging feeling grows inside of you, that sense that you are not making a difference any more – that's the hardest. You are a champion with no one to champion and a budget deficit to address. *Where* is the last kid you championed? *Who* was the last kid you championed? This can hit you like a train. It certainly did me. This wasn't what I was meant to be.

Ah, the waiting place. It's definitely not a good place. You might be here for some time. You won't be alone though. You will hear lots of tiny voices here. Listen out for them and, when you hear them, listen hard. They will help you find your way out; they helped me find mine. One day, while I was in the waiting place, a tiny voice spoke to me: 'Hey, I've got this kid … he never has a clean uniform on, and he always has his head down. I've tried everything.'

Wait a second, I know the answer to this one. My hand shoots up. Hey! I know, I know! For a while, the other tiny voices are hushed. They are waiting to hear what you have to say. When you finish, another tiny voice speaks out: 'Well, I've got this kid, she's always on her own, she doesn't seem to have any friends. I'm running out of things to try.'

Then it dawns on you. Every child does need a champion, but so does every teacher! Yes, of course Rita, you're right, but you could go further:

Every teacher deserves a champion – a mentor who will never give up on them, who understands the power of connections and insists that they become the best that they can possibly be.

You prepare to leave the waiting place. You're feeling better already. Now your real work begins again. You were a great champion before and you can do it again. But to be a champion again, you need to find that individual to champion. So, you pick your teachers. The one who puts you through your paces every day. The one who always forgets there's a staff meeting. The one who never hands in their data on time. The one who takes on too much and the one who doesn't take on enough. The one you have to remind to do their marking. The one who comes to the door looking sad last thing on a Friday just when you've picked up your handbag and car keys.

It's been a while since I left the waiting place. There is a heartfelt card on my mantelpiece from one of the teachers I championed who has since left to take up a headship of her own. (It is next to the heartfelt card from the mother of one of the F-bomb kids I championed who has just sat his GCSEs.) Before she left, she asked me the secret to being a champion:

1. **Rule 1: Listen. Listen hard. Do not interrupt**

   Listen to others and listen to yourself. Cut out the noise for just a while. Let thinking happen. In the words of Nancy Kline, 'interruption diminishes us, diminishes our thinking'.[2] Allow time to process thoughts and reflections before you react. Be comfortable with silence. Pause. Then do the right thing, the thing your own tiny voices have you told you about.

2. **Rule 2: Be caring but stern**

   Wanting another to be all they can be, to be better than they are now, is no easy job. You need to care, really care. And caring often means doing the opposite of what they want you to do. They might want you to be easy on them, to make them feel good, especially when things aren't working out, but that can be counterproductive. Research highlights the importance of being both 'caring' and 'stern',[3]

---

2   Nancy Kline, *The Promise That Changes Everything: I Won't Interrupt You* (London: Penguin Random House, 2020).

3   Robert Garvey, David Megginson and Paul Stokes, *Coaching and Mentoring: Theory and Practice* (London: Sage, 2010), p. 13.

creating an environment where knowing what to do emerges through 'dialogue, systematic questioning and participation in critical debate'.[4] Tough love is still love.

3. **Rule 3: Be vulnerable**

In another well-watched video with much for teachers to take away, self-esteem guru Brené Brown reassures us that it's OK to be vulnerable:

> Vulnerability is not about winning or losing. It's having the courage to show up even when you can't control the outcome.[5]

As a mentor, you are not in control. You do not know how a conversation is going to start, let alone end. It's not only OK to say, 'I don't know', it's vital. You are a champion, not a god. 'I don't know so let's find out' sends as powerful a message to an adult as it does to a child. We are all learners, and learning is important.

Being a champion, whether for a child or an adult, is what makes your role worthwhile, whether you are a first-year teacher or an educator rather longer in the tooth. Who are you going to champion?

If you are a school leader you need a champion too. You need a champion *especially* if you are school leader. So, who is your champion?

Emma Courtney is an assistant head teacher and mentor in Luton Primary School, Chatham. She is also a master's student at Canterbury Christ Church University.

---

4   Haili Hughes, *Mentoring in Schools: How to Become an Expert Colleague – Aligned with the Early Career Framework* (Carmarthen: Crown House Publishing, 2021), p. 11.
5   Brené Brown, The power of vulnerability [video], *TED* (June 2010). Available at: https://www.ted.com/talks/brene_brown_the_power_of_vulnerability?language=en.

Chapter 5

The Power of Lightbulb Moments

Debbie Furgueson

I love a lightbulb moment. You sometimes see them when you teach children. You often see them when children are learning for themselves. That moment of discovery, of finding out, when you see their eyes light up, is a moment every educator loves. The more lightbulb moments, the more our children are growing, personally as well as academically.

Creating student-run after-school volunteer clubs help to create just such lightbulb moments.

The first club I started was when I was teaching at elementary school. I was in the wealthiest county in the state, and most children there lived in great privilege. Many had horses, went on trips and cruises regularly, wore nothing but designer clothing and so on. Of course, there is nothing wrong with having nice things, but it was clear by how they spoke that they were unaware that not everyone lived like this. There is a difference between 'want' and 'need', and I could see they did not understand this difference.

One day, I overheard one of my fifth-graders telling a classmate, 'I told my mom I wanted a *white* iPhone … and she got me a *black* one! I made her take it back!' I'll never forget it. It was October 2008 and that model had been out for only a month. This 10-year-old boy was complaining about the color of a brand-new cell phone he had been given.

That was the proverbial last straw for me. They needed a lesson in appreciation – both for what they had and for the fact that not everyone else was in the same lucky boat. Most people do not enjoy the life advantages they did, and that was a lesson they needed to learn quickly.

Something that had always bugged me was how schools would only collect food for the disadvantaged around the holidays, as if people weren't going hungry every day of the year. I wanted my students to recognize that if people are hungry, if they don't have enough food for their families, this isn't a 'holiday-only' happening. It's an everyday occurrence and something we need to do something about, every day. It was time to act.

With a plan in mind, I went to our local grocery store and picked up 50 handheld baskets that were earmarked for the trash, which they were kind enough to 'lend' me. Taking them home, I made labels for each one, and the following Monday morning every member of staff came into school to find a basket bearing their name outside their door. The Antler Pantry was now open.[1]

The way it worked was simple. On any given day, children could bring in donations of non-perishables and put them in their teacher's basket for my students to go around and collect. Soon, there were so many items of food generously brought in that my classroom was bulging at the seams, so the school principal let me use an empty classroom and a parent donated a dozen industrial storage shelves. The Antler Pantry now had its own premises!

My kids took such pride in keeping it organized, and before long it looked like a mini grocery store. They were genuinely excited when they saw an empty space where an item had been, as they knew it meant someone, somewhere was being helped. Seeing them make flyers to hang around school to ask for more cereal or cookies or diapers showed me that they were really focused on making sure everything needed was fully 'in stock'. And, importantly, they did this of their own accord – child-centered learning and activism in action. You could have lit the Antler Pantry by the lightbulb moments they were having.

Within 2 years, our Antler Pantry was feeding people across over half the county. A need that had been invisible was no longer unseen. And when

---

1   Our school mascot was a moose, so why not?

I saw 'cell phone boy' explaining to a new student how we had the Antler Pantry because people were hungry 'all year round' and that we needed to help others when we could, I knew the message had hit home.

This project led to others, like raising money for the Red Cross after hurricanes, designing a scholarship funded by a faculty spelling bee and helping during the Special Olympics. Doing good endures too. Once you start, you can't stop. These activities are still taking place at the school over a decade later.

For me, the most important result of this work wasn't just that students 'got it' – that they developed a new awareness of the real challenges others had to deal with on a daily basis – it was that these students saw how they could take action to make things better. They could make a difference. They could be the change.

Helping privileged students to see poverty and hunger is one thing, but how do you address issues of need when the children you are working with are the ones in need themselves?

My next post was in a different county and at a Title I school.[2] I had now moved from the wealthiest county in the state to one of the poorest, and a different approach would be the order of the day.

Need was not something hidden to my new students. It was the life they lived daily. The main issue here was addressing that sense of powerlessness that anyone can succumb to when life beats you down day after day. The same need for student-centered learning and lightbulb moments existed here. I just needed a different plan.

This time I headed to my local home improvement store and cajoled them into 'lending' me a box of flowerpots. I had my students paint them in bright colors and then pot them up for us to take to the seniors' center down the road. Next, we managed to get a major fabric store to give us some spare rolls of fleece and the kids made scarves to give out to the

---

2   Title I is a federal education programme that supports low-income students throughout the US. Funds are distributed to high-poverty schools, as determined by the number of students who qualify for free or reduced lunch (see https://cces. washk12.org/what-does-it-mean-to-be-a-title-i-school/#:~:text=WHAT%20 IS%20A%20TITLE%20I,for%20free%20or%20reduced%20lunch).

homeless. Another time we cleaned up a corner park that had become an eyesore and was attracting the wrong sort of visitors.

We decided to call our various projects Love Grows – and, oh my, how it has! The students are now finding other projects and working creatively – and cooperatively – to find solutions with, of course, those lightbulb moments left, right and center.

You see, volunteerism for students, especially when projects are suggested and designed by them, creates such amazing internalizations. Pride in self. Pride in community. Feelings of empowerment. I would encourage every educator to develop student volunteerism at their school. Empathy is increased. Creative problem solving is improved. Self-confidence blossoms. All this as a result of children learning to think outside of themselves. These are life skills that know no income bracket, race, religion or zip code. What's more, the positive effects carry over into classes, so you improve your academics too!

Debbie Furgueson is the founder and CEO of A Better Classroom and lives in New London, Connecticut. Her work is founded on research and is all about keeping relationships, empathy and achievement at the forefront of education. A Better Classroom has trained over 500 educators and its strength lies in strong background knowledge as well as experience in trauma response, positive behaviour interventions and supports, and restorative practices.

Chapter 6

It's Not What You Think

Liz Stevenson

All the teachers looked the same and I even got sixth formers confused with teachers

Year 6 child after a transition visit to a secondary school

Over the years as a transition manager for a local authority in the Midlands, I have had the privilege – and it is a real privilege – of talking to children from Years 5 to 8 about their transition from primary school to secondary. What comes though time and time again is that the concerns they have about this important but daunting event in their young lives are not the concerns that we, as adults, think they have. And the problems they went on to experience once they had made the transition were not the problems they had been for prepared for anyway.

Drawing on those insightful, surprising and sometimes shocking conversations, I would like to share some insights I have learned from children, in seven key areas, as they make that move from primary school to secondary.

1. Talking to new people is hard

Regardless of whether this is with a new teacher or a new peer, starting a conversation with someone for the first time is a skill that many children (and adults!) simply haven't mastered.

Leave a group of three or four 12-year-olds in a room together for the first time and see what happens. I suggest very little, to begin with at least. Many, if not most children have never been in a situation where they have to make small talk with new people. It's a daunting prospect, one that makes an awkward silence the lesser of two evils.

So how can you help?

Teach them how to engage new people in conversation, no matter how small the talk. Show them how it's done. It's a great life skill and falls neatly in the 'social capital' box. Model to them how to ask questions and take an interest in new people. Remember, too, to show them how to answer. Monosyllables do not a conversation make. It's easy to assume children are always happy to share insights into their lives, but the reality is that this is not always the case. Not straightaway anyway.

If you are a primary school teacher, start to encourage children talk to new people. Help them identify situations where they can get into this habit. Using pupils to meet and greet and to show guests around the school is a great way of building skills and confidence when it comes to small talk.

If you are in a secondary school, help the children get into this habit by being the one to show them how it's done. Bring guests into school from all walks of life and make sure your students get to spend time talking *with* them, not just listening to them.

The level of social pressure felt by children at the start of Year 7 is immense. You probably get that, looking at it through your adult eyes – but if you are 11 years old, it is genuinely *immense*. Just letting them know that you understand this is a concern for them is a great place to start.

2. What if …?

Starting a new school is full of so many 'what ifs'. What if I'm not in the same class as my friends? What if I'm in a class with people I don't like? What if I forget my books? What if I'm late for school? What if I get lost? Ask a class for their most pressing 'what ifs' and you'll end up with twice as many suggestions as there are children. And that's just the things they are prepared to mention. They'll be worrying about even more things they daren't tell you about.

Because most of these 'what ifs' are groundless, it's all too easy to dismiss them with a 'You'll be fine' because, overall, they will be. But that's not the point. We know that the children will adapt very quickly and will find their new flow, but when you're aged 10 or 11, it can be hard to see your way to that position. What's more, the more they are dismissed with an 'Oh, you'll be fine', the less they will confide in you in the future. Their concerns are genuine and need to be heard.

Children have said to me many times that the adults in their lives told them that secondary school would be different, but that no one explained how! What children need is for you to be their advocate, to be their voice and to help them find their own. They need you to work with them to address all of their concerns. This is the biggest change many of them will have ever been through and they need your help to guide them through it.

3. Lunchtimes and break

The change of systems and plans during secondary school lunches and breaktimes is a huge shock to the system. One story that always sticks with me is from talking to a group of boys in Year 7. They told me how for the first week or so in their new school, they hadn't eaten any lunch. They had been going off to play football when lunch started at 1 p.m. as they knew that Year 7 could go to the canteen at 1.15 p.m. Each day, though, before they knew it, they missed their time slot, only realising this when they heard the bell ringing to mark the end of their lunchtime! It turns out they had been waiting for the dinner staff to come out and ring the hand bell to signal it was time for them to line up to enter the canteen. Of course, this does not happen in most secondary schools, but this was the system they were used to and no one had told them it would be any different.

What is noteworthy here, too, is that this all took place after the school had given the new children an extended lunch break to get used to how the canteen was run and help them practise the habit of choosing not only what food to eat, but which of the three outlets to buy it from. I found out about this by simply asking the children. You can do this too. They will give you insights you may well have missed, no matter how empathetic you are.

Talking of school lunches, the first year at secondary school is often the first time many children will have had to budget properly. Practising this important life skill with them will be time well spent, alleviating worries and helping them make choices that are good for their well-being as well as their purse.

4. Time management

Ask any child how much control they have over their own timekeeping at primary school and you will more often than not find the answer is none whatsoever! They are escorted to school by an adult, handed over (gratefully) to an adult, guided in and out of lesson times and school spaces by an adult and eventually handed (gratefully) back to an adult at the end of the day. The need to be in charge of their own time management the minute they hit Year 7 can come as quite a shock.

What are you doing to help them learn the skills needed to get themselves to the right place at the right time (and with the right kit)?

And while we're on the subject of time management, a quick word about bells. At primary school, a bell usually means stop playing and line up. At secondary it's to tell the teachers when to stop teaching or tell the pupils they need to be already lining up outside a classroom door. The difference is significant for children, so let's help them with it.

5. Homework

Over the years, pupils in Year 7 have told me that the new expectations around the homework itself are not a huge problem. What is a challenge, however, is the organisation and time management needed to do it – to do it well and do it on time.

In primary they may well be used to having homework given once a week, which is handed in on a set day. The class teacher is there to remind/encourage/nag them about these expectations. There is also often the expectation, implicit or otherwise, that parents will be there to help.

Compared to that system, the homework policies of most secondary schools are like a game of chess. Three pieces of work on a Monday, one of which to be handed in on Wednesday, one on Friday and one the following Monday. Three more on Tuesday, all of which are to be handed in on Tuesday of the following week. Wednesday sees two pieces: one for Friday and one for Tuesday. You get the picture. And the only thing to nag the children is a folded-up homework timetable in their blazer pocket that not all teachers stick to anyway.

Using planners and homework diaries – or even, increasingly, an online system – is useful, of course, but this is often a completely new way of working and children need time and help to develop the habit of using these systems, as well as adapting to the new demands of the size and breadth of homework expected of them.

6. Who is who?

Something that Year 6 children have often told me they worry about is moving from a school where they know everyone, and everyone knows them, to a setting where pretty much everyone is a stranger.

Remember your first day at school as a teacher? The nightmares you had in the build up to it? Starting at a new school is a daunting prospect for us as grown-ups, unless we are supremely confident or just don't care. Combine this fear of something new and scary with my first point about how hard it can be to talk to new people. An induction day is great, but that's all it is – a day. And a day is never enough time to learn who is who. Again, remember being shown around your school on your first day and being introduced to all those new people. At the end of the day, it's all just a blur anyway.

Like the child quoted at the top of this chapter, it's hard to remember who is who. Here is another plea from one Year 7 I spoke to: 'If you're going to use photos of staff to help us get used to what they look like, can schools make sure they are up to date? I didn't recognise a few in real life, they looked so different in the photo.' While this may seem a fairly obvious request, it's something many schools neglect to do.

7. Being an appropriate version of yourself

Working out who you are and how you fit in your environment is always tricky, not only for children but for teachers too. I have saved this point until last because, while I hope that everything I have mentioned so far has given you food for thought, this is something that must be discussed openly with children (and staff). In my experience such discussion is possibly the most important way to ensure a smooth transition.

If you teach children in the first year after their arrival at 'big school', have you ever found yourself despairing that these children just don't know how to behave in a lesson? My conversations with them suggest that often it is because they do not know the new 'rules of the game' and are simply doing what they used to do in Year 6. This not only relates to actions such as moving from their seats without permission or helping themselves to resources without asking, but also knowing where the boundaries lie when it comes to being funny or knowing when the time is right – or otherwise – to be a bit cheeky.

I suggest that often they are not behaving badly. Rather, they are being themselves. I have never suggested a child ever change themselves for teachers. What I do say is that they need to find the appropriate version of themselves for their audience (i.e. the teacher).

For this approach to be given the best chance of success, the teacher needs to understand that finding the appropriate version of themselves will take some time. A child who is labelled 'naughty' in week one will have trouble shaking that off, especially when you may only see that child once or twice a week anyway. Remember too that children are learning the quirks, tolerances, expectations and red lines of perhaps up to 15 new teachers, all in a week or so. High expectations are important, of course, but realism, patience and understanding in the face of a class of disoriented 11-year-olds is important too.

*

I hope I have given you some idea of the challenges that children go through during transition and how you can help. I have spent a great deal of time talking to children about this stage of their school lives, but there is no need to take my word for it because your situation might be different. All I ask is that you do what I have done – sit down with them and talk to them about their concerns and experiences. Listen openly and then act on what you hear. After all, even small changes can make for a great transition.

In 21 years in education, Liz Stevenson has worked in primary, secondary and special schools. As a Key Stage 3 pastoral lead and primary-trained teacher, she soon developed an interest in transition from primary to secondary education and is fortunate enough to have been a transition manager for a local authority. She now works in school improvement in the heart of the Midlands.

Chapter 7

Trauma-Informed Practice: Knowing Then Doing

Sheila Mulvenney

As a nurse, then later as a teacher, I am very glad that we know better now than we did centuries or even decades ago. But sadly, in my experience, there are still many ways in which we, as teachers, can do better.

The good news is that our understanding of how children learn has developed a great deal. For example, we now recognise that cognitive load – the amount of information that the memory can work with at any one time – has an impact on learning, and this is hopefully reflected in the way learning activities are planned and presented.

Less positively, we still have a way to go to fully integrate other aspects of our knowledge about learning into common practice. We know these things, it's just that we are yet to use what we know and, as a wise man once said, 'To know and not to do is really not to know.'[1]

I would like to use my tiny voice to suggest one important area where we need more quickly to make the transition from knowing to doing in our

---

1   Stephen R. Covey, *The 7 Habits of Highly Effective People* (New York: Simon & Schuster, 1989), p. 12.

professional practice: understanding the impact of trauma and attachment in the classroom.

We now understand much more than we once did about the many ways in which trauma, attachment and early adversity impact the brain. This means we have a much better insight into the actions, behaviours and choices of the children and young people in our schools. We know, for example, that early adversity impacts physically the development of the amygdala – the part of our brain that acts as an alarm system for our survival response. Children who have experienced early adversity often have an enlarged amygdala.[2]

Issues around attachment can also lead to a range of issues that might show in a child's behaviour.[3] Essentially, if babies and children enjoy a strong positive attachment with their caregiver(s) – carers who meet their needs with consistency – they are better able to grow up with a sense of safety, to trust adults and to form relationships.

What this all means for educators

What if you reframed a child's attention-seeking behaviour as attachment-seeking behaviour? How might that change your responses? A child in need of attachment wants to know that you, as an adult, have noticed them. They need to know that you will keep them safe, that they can trust you and feel secure with you and that, if necessary, you will step in to soothe them and help them learn to soothe themselves as they mature.

That child who persistently asks questions, who constantly wants to be reassured, who demands close proximity to you as an adult, perhaps always wanting to do jobs for you, to please you – that's the child who may well be seeking attachment.

---

2   Jamie L. Hanson and Brendon M. Nacewicz, Amygdala allostasis and early life adversity: considering excitotoxicity and inescapability in the sequelae of stress, *Frontiers in Human Neuroscience* 15 (2021): 624705. DOI 10.3389/fnhum.2021.624705.

3   Louise Bomber, *Inside I'm Hurting: Practical Strategies for Supporting Children with Attachment Difficulties in Schools* (London: Worth Publishing, 2007).

Attachment is a deep need within all humans. We can die of a lack of it. A human baby needs an adult to claim them and meet their needs. If these needs haven't been met in the home or when they are babies, they don't simply disappear by walking into your classroom. The child's strongest driver, stronger than the drive to behave or learn what your curriculum says they should be learning, will be to have their attachment needs met. Meet those needs – help all children to feel safe and secure, to know that they belong and are loved – and then you have children who are ready to learn.

> If children feel safe, they can take risks, ask questions, make mistakes, learn to trust, share their feelings and grow.[4]

For children who have experienced trauma in early life, with the attendant toxic stress which causes changes in the way the brain develops, the classroom can feel a very scary place. They may be hyper alert to threat and danger, may be so used to living in fear and chaos, often without the mitigating impact of close attachments with adults who can protect and reassure, that they can hardly recognise what 'calm' feels like. Such children may be judged as 'overreacting' to minor incidents and their behaviour can be seen as defiance, aggression, running away or hiding, becoming withdrawn or disengaged.[5] If adults respond in ways that are confrontational or punitive, this is likely to fuel this response still further. What these children need is help in calming and regulating.

We don't punish the child who can't yet read or write or do fractions – we teach them how, with care and patience. Punishing a child who has not had the experiences they need to regulate their emotions is both cruel and counterproductive. None of us is born able to regulate or soothe ourselves. We learn these important skills by first learning to co-regulate with an adult. This is something that happened each and every time we were distressed as a baby, picked up by a calm adult and soothed. Without this, or enough of this, we will not learn to self-regulate or self-soothe. For a child, this means that when they are overwhelmed by emotions such as anger,

---

4   Alfie Kohn, *Punished by Rewards*, 25th anniversary edn (London: Mariner Books, 2018).

5   Anna Freud NCCF, Childhood trauma and the brain | UK Trauma Council [video], *YouTube* (27 September 2020). Available at: https://www.youtube.com/watch?v=xYBUY1kZpf8.

frustration, fear or anxiety, regardless of your thoughts and judgements on the matter, they may well 'lose it'.

So, what can we do to support these children?

- Get to know the children and young people we work with well – not just their academic scores or potential.

- Ask the designated teacher or designated safeguarding team about those who may have experienced issues with attachment, trauma or adversity.

- Do what we can to ensure that children feel safe in our classrooms (predictability, approachability and being prepared to listen all help).

- View developing genuine relationships with children as important.

- Devote time to relationships – a warm welcome (sharing information, remembering their likes and dislikes, smiling and having fun) doesn't need to take long but can really help.

- Recognise the warning signs of dysregulation and intervene quickly with support and calmness.

- Over time, teach them about what happens when they dysregulate, and find the things that help them regulate.

One final word. While perennial behaviour management notions of 'consistency' and 'boundaries' are important, they will never aid the healing process for children whose greatest needs are attachment, learning to trust adults and learning to self-regulate. Schools that know this do not enforce one-size-fits-all behaviour policies on all children (and their teachers). What they do with this knowledge is to make sure they are consistently caring and compassionate, making reasonable adjustments to meet the needs of all children.

After working for many years in both care (as a nurse and then health visitor) and a variety of education settings, including being head of virtual school for Children in Care, Sheila Mulvenney now spends the majority of her time training other professionals in trauma and attachment, phonics and well-being.

Chapter 8

Batons of Discovery

Verity Saunders

I knew from an early age that I wanted to be a doctor. So, it seems like I was the only one surprised when I ended up in education, as everyone else had told me that being a teacher was 'clearly' what I was born to do. I am pleased, however, that my journey has led to me to the classroom where I sit and write these words now, proud of what I have achieved. Over the course of that journey, I have made a number of discoveries which I endeavour to pass on to the children I teach, baton-like, in the hope that they will share them with their children in turn.

This is me using my tiny voice to share these batons of discovery with you too.

Baton 1: Tenacity is a virtue

I now understand that my journey of discovery began when I was 4. I just didn't realise it then. What I was unwavering about, even then, was that I wanted to be a doctor.

In my classes, I see the spark of hopes and dreams in even the youngest children I teach. I am determined to support them in their journey by encouraging them to aim high, dream big and go for what it is they want. They may be young, but who am I to say they don't know their own mind? Never underestimate small humans! In my lessons I ensure there is time for them to express their ideas, thoughts and feelings, tricky though that can be with a tightly packed curriculum and an even more crammed time-table. For me, the importance of promoting self-awareness, self-confidence and the pursuit of one's own passion cannot be underestimated.

It's lovely to see children actively encouraging each other as each new class comes together, and the visible boost to the children's self-esteem, intrinsic motivation and independence this brings. My mantra is 'see, believe and encourage', and I need to really see each child in my class, show them I believe in them and encourage each and every one to have a dream and follow it.

When I was 16, still very much intent on being a doctor, my chemistry teacher took me to one side to tell me that I was not good enough or clever enough to pursue a career in medicine. Maybe he was right; we'll never know. Regardless of what he thought or why he thought it, I left his class-room crushed, with my one dream in tatters. The heartbreak I felt was real and it was devastating. My life's drive, the motivational force that got me up in the morning, stopped. My greatest fear was that he was right. My greatest regret was that maybe he wasn't.

After many tears came some serious soul-searching and a process of re-evaluation. I was down but not out. I bounced back with a new focus and a renewed sense of determination. The road had not ended; it had just changed. Tenacity – with its roots in 'holding fast' and, further back, 'to stretch' – truly is a virtue.

Baton 2: We need to learn – and teach – emotional resilience

The words of my chemistry teacher resonated within me for quite some time. My nemesis became self-doubt. My new-found levels of tenacity, however, meant I was all the more determined to succeed: to do so via a new journey, to do it for myself and, yes, to prove him wrong. What I learned at that time was that I held a deep inner strength that I didn't know I had – something I could draw upon whenever it was needed. It meant I knew that, when it came to it, I could handle more than I had once thought – and that was a bit like having a little superpower. I could do anything, just not teaching, thank you very much.

Over the past decade, I have witnessed a dip in the emotional resilience of the children I have taught. In too many, the fearless innocence of hope and self-belief seems to have been replaced by a deep-seated fear of failure – the ceaseless, debilitating worry that they are not good enough and just can't do it, whatever the 'it' is. I discovered my inner strength and self-belief the hard way, and I strive to help the children I teach to find theirs too, but hopefully in a more creative and compassionate way.

For better or for worse, we educators are also influencers and role models in our schools. As such, the power of our words and actions cannot be underestimated. Children see and hear everything – something that is especially important when you remember that what you do often speaks louder than what you say. Model emotional resilience. Share your attempts that ended up as failures, as well as your successes. Talk about how the things that excite you also make you scared. Show them how success is not what you achieve but being true to how you are.

For a while, I lived my life not as a doctor but not yet a teacher, and then suddenly it happened. I woke up one morning and realised they were right all along. It was clear now: I *was* born to do it.

It was time to become a teacher. And the clue had been in the name all along.

Baton 3: Be your authentic self

I moved into teaching in 2003. I have no regrets and I love life in the classroom with my small humans. What is more, I use aspects of my previous career as a trainee clinical psychologist every single day. The word 'verity' (my name) means 'truth', and the person my children see every day is me – the true, authentic, real me.

You being you in the classroom is so important. That way, the you the children see, connect with and remember is the real you. And, in that way, you help them be them. Providing a safe space for them to express themselves, without fear of judgement, is so important. I want each and every child to be valued, heard, respected and treated fairly as an individual in their own right.

I regularly need to remind myself that I am enough. Being me and being open and honest about it, is what it takes. I believe it is vital to try to articulate my thoughts, modelling how to overcome mistakes and showing how to attempt something new, even if it goes wrong (especially if it goes wrong!), is empowering to my children. By me being enough, I can help them know that they are enough too. Children need someone to have their back – to champion them, as we have heard elsewhere. And it is such a privilege to hold that position in their lives. It may be only briefly, but it is something they will carry with them all their lives.

So, if 'verity' means 'truth', what is the truth? Who is Verity? I am just me. I am not my job title, or the things I do or what I have done. I am a mother, daughter, wife, sister, niece, friend, cousin, teacher, leader, and I wouldn't change any of that. These things are part of what shapes me. But these nouns do not define who I am. Discovering who you are as a person, knowing it and owning it, both personally and professionally, is powerfully liberating. Don't get me wrong, it's something I need to keep working on. But I am me, and that's enough.

My job in the classroom is to put children front and centre and help them identify, strive for and go on to achieve their potential, while having the courage to be honest with them and their parents in a positive and nurturing way to help them flourish. I want each and every one of the children in my care to know that they are enough, and that they need to live their lives for themselves, not to please others. They deserve to know that, and I see it as part of my job to pass that important message – that baton – on to them.

I am a teacher, eventually. I wear my heart on my sleeve, and what you see is what you get. Imposter syndrome often creeps in professionally, but with age, a confidence has begun to grow. I love being a teacher. You should too.

Verity Saunders has been teaching in the early years foundation stage and Key Stage 1 for almost 20 years. She never thought she was going to become a teacher, and little did she know that the road to discovery would be so scenic.

Part II
Tiny Voices Talk About Teaching

I'm going to be controversial.

Yes, I know that I said that I was quite a 'beige' child and I have even been described as 'beige' on Twitter before. Just because I don't air my views all the time, however, doesn't mean that I don't have them. I just wait until I feel safe to share them, and I do so here. I am among friends, on pages that are devoted to tiny voices sharing strong opinions and I know that you will hear me out. You may not agree, but you will hear.

Controversial point 1: It really bothers me that, as professionals, we are given perfect lesson formats and told to teach like the teacher next door. We are professionals and should be allowed to develop our craft. I don't believe that anyone expected Frida Kahlo to paint like Claude Monet, so why does this happen in teaching? Considering the English educational system, I wonder if it is due to the omnipresent nature of Ofsted that looms over every educational establishment. Do leaders give teachers the 'perfect lesson plan' to follow in the hope that the Ofsted hurdle will be jumped effortlessly? Yes, I know it isn't as simple as that, but it annoys me.

Over my more than two decades of teaching, I have been lucky enough to see many teachers teach, but something has dawned on me as the years have moved on: I am me. I can't teach like you and you can't teach like me because we are all different. Different is not bad in teaching; in fact, for the young people in our schools it is possibly incredibly refreshing. Imagine going through your entire school life being taught by clones! Going back to Kahlo, she didn't feel she needed to paint like Monet; she felt able to express herself in her own way and we need to teach in the way that works for us. We need to be trusted to be the professionals we are.

Controversial point 2: We have a duty to keep learning. No, I don't mean just attend the weekly staff meetings, I mean truly learn our craft. Virtuoso pianists still have lessons, yet many teachers stop choosing to learn and develop their craft after they become qualified. The way I teach today doesn't resemble how I taught 20 years ago and, if I'm honest, it doesn't even resemble the way I taught 3 years ago. Teaching moves on and as professionals we have to remain informed. Our professional development (which is covered in later chapters) should be informed by our passion for teaching and not by what the leadership team are telling us we need to be learning that year.

Great teachers often have piles of books devoted to their craft and there are so many wonderful books out there at the moment. What do you want to learn more about? What is your passion within teaching? Write it down and then find out more about it. The next few chapters are devoted to just this – teachers sharing their passion for teaching. We have the voices of educators from early years to further education and all have powerful points to share.

There we go – I tried not to be beige and it didn't hurt too much. I will leave you on this note: after all these years I still love teaching, and I am sure it is because I am authentically me in my classroom and I love learning about my craft. So, be you and learn lots!

Chapter 9

The 'Why' in EYFS

Kim Peacock

Whatever your role in the early years foundation stage (EYFS), whether you're a brand-new classroom teacher or a longer-in-the-tooth senior leadership team member like me, always remember there's a 'why' in EYFS.

Every child is different, which makes every context different. What works for me today may not work for you. It might not even work for me tomorrow! It's easy to fall into the trap of adopting new policy and practice without asking why. What drives you in your context and how will the proposed changes take you closer? I'm not suggesting you should be resistant to change. I'm simply saying we should all have the professional courage to stop and ask the big questions before we go through the mental and emotional challenge of bringing in new things. And the biggest question of all is the little matter of why.

Before you think about what you might want to change *to*, you really need to understand what you are changing *from*. This starts with observation and research *in situ*. Spend time in your EYFS provision watching what is happening and understanding – and then embracing – what makes your setting unique. What are your strengths and how can you turn any possible weaknesses into future triumphs? As a start, work your way through the following three early years principles and take time to reflect on how each supports the children, adults, parents, school and even the wider community.

Positive relationships

How do the children, adults and parents interact? How are the needs of all the stakeholders being identified and then met? Is the practice inclusive and respectful of everybody's needs? How is equity achieved for children, staff and families, all of whom may have very different starting points? For example, what does transition look like and how is everyone's voice heard in this process? And how does it vary, if at all, depending on the time of year it takes place?

The same principles can be applied to how you support new staff members entering your setting; does this vary depending on their role, experience and subject knowledge? How do you make the most of the added skills and knowledge they bring to the team while also helping them learn your routines and practices and, especially, your particular 'why'?

Enabling environments

How are children and practitioners encouraged to become independent, resilient learners who know how to manage risk? How do the resources in the environment support and encourage potential learning opportunities? Do the children know how to use the resources within the continuous provision? Has the process been carefully scaffolded on a one-to-one basis, then in small groups, then supervised from a distance and then with the children operating independently, applying the skills they have learned in different contexts? For example, in September we strip back our creative provision, then rebuild it in response to the children's specific interests, abilities and knowledge. Many of the children who enter our setting may not have experienced self-service playdough or a paint station (with powder paint and water in a drinks dispenser, which they manipulate to make their own paint) in their feeder setting, or cool melt glue guns, which we introduce to add challenges and develop their knowledge and skills (and our ability to tolerate mess!).

The same principles can also be applied to adults in our setting. How do we upskill our staff to ensure they have the subject knowledge and confidence to evolve as professionals? How do we encourage and nurture them to apply the skills they have learned? Roll up your sleeves and get down on the children's level – literally and metaphorically – and watch how they engage with the provision on offer and how it all comes together to support their learning.

Learning and development

Does practice in your setting have the children at the centre of it and is it responsive to what children know but also how they learn? Do children have an opportunity to access a broad and balanced curriculum which is purposeful and promotes the characteristics of effective learning? What is the research and pedagogy that underpins how your curriculum is designed and how it is being implemented? For instance, the children who enter our setting typically have poor fine motor skills; therefore, while we have a discrete fine motor skills area within our provision, there are opportunities to develop these skills throughout it. This is especially important as not all children will choose to engage with this area when it might suit us. You will see pipettes in the creative and water-tray areas, wooden tongs in our self-service snack area (which the children use when operating the toaster) and miniature containers, scoops and small shells in our indoor sand provision so the children can develop their muscles and coordination in a variety of contexts.

We also recognise, as a team, that we have to invest in developing the gross motor skills that are essential if children are to acquire fine motor skills. This means there are lots of opportunities for the children to develop these skills, from climbing ladders in our outdoor area ('taking managed risks') to using giant mops, giant paintbrushes on the end of broom handles and giant sponges to wash our bikes.

Every time we add new resources to our environment, the team carefully thinks about the 'why' behind them.[1] We are then better placed to reflect on the impact the changes have.

We are passionately child-centred but, of course, there will be times when direct teaching is what's needed when it comes to developing certain skills, and we build opportunities for this into our daily routines. For example, when the children arrive at school, they self-register using photographs of

---

1   And this is never 'Because Ofsted'.

45

themselves and put them on a 'tens' frame to discuss later as they develop their knowledge of mathematical concepts. They also write their names in an A4 diary to develop fine motor skills and name-writing.

Of course, these same principles can also be applied to our staff. How do we support them to grow as practitioners? There are moments when we need to invest time and money so they can access external training linked to either individual need or particular aspects of new practice we are introducing; however, there are also times when actually having open dialogue and allowing them to just watch other members of staff in the team is equally valuable. In addition, we have created a 'We are practitioners' display that reflects our culture and ethos, with quotes to inspire and a variety of books for practitioners to use for their own research.

Ask your EYFS team what research and pedagogy inspires their practice and, of course, why. There is no right or wrong answer here and our team is not averse to cherry-picking the practice to fit our needs. Sometimes we adopt something in its purest form and other times we adapt, spending time thinking about how we can make it fit our specific needs. Walk around our EYFS setting and you'll see a splatter-and-splodge approach – a bit of one approach and a lot of another – all the time justified and monitored by our 'why'.

Once you have invested time in observing and researching before you bring in changes, it is vital to move from 'why' to 'what'. Be fleet-footed here too. It's not all about big whole-school changes. Stay alert and respond quickly to the needs that suddenly appear in front of you, especially the unexpected ones. For example, if the children really seem to enjoy making marks on the floor in other areas of the provision and have become fascinated with the construction process of their buildings but are not engaging with the clipboards provided, try adding large pieces of squared paper to the construction area for them to use.

Brand-new provocations can be added relatively cheaply too. How about a pop-up 'tinker tray' – a treasure trove of old electrical items from parents and local businesses, stored on a temporary stand made from recycled pallets with a few borrowed safety goggles and screwdrivers from the design technology resource cupboard? That's a good start, but your 'why' will be what determines what happens next. For instance, our tinker tray has now transformed into a woodwork station that includes a bench with vices, a variety of different tools – from Japanese wood saws to hand drills – wood, safety equipment and accessories.

To get here, the team considered our 'why' and decided we needed to challenge our children to extend their learning and develop their skills further. We then invested time in researching how to make this happen so staff had the right subject knowledge and children had the correct equipment for it to have the impact we intended. Consequently, we now have children truly taking the lead in their learning and applying many of the skills they have learned in all areas of the curriculum when they plan, measure and make their designs. It has been fascinating to watch how their ideas and skills have evolved over time, and it has proven to be an amazing addition to our setting.

You too will be amazed how liberating it is – and how creative you will all become – when you spend time on the 'why' in EYFS.

Kim Peacock is an assistant head teacher and EYFS leader of a two-form entry primary school on the Yorkshire coast. She has a history degree and Postgraduate Certificate in Education in early years (3 to 7). Her experience and background in a variety of settings and leadership roles has shaped her current practice and she is passionate about play-based learning.

Chapter 10

Getting the Most out of PSHE

Pauline Stirling

You might know it as personal, social and health education (PSHE), health education and relationships education (HERE) or relationships and sex education (RSE). You might be delivering it as a class teacher or as a tutor. You might be delivering it in form time, pastoral time or tutor time, or as part of a weekly or fortnightly timetabled curriculum slot. You may even be lucky enough to have a subject specialist to deliver it.

Any teacher who has been handed a pile of photocopies with blurry pictures of the human reproductive system (or a cucumber and a condom) will know that feeling of 'This isn't what I signed up for!' You may feel you lack up-to-date knowledge or are concerned about stretching your classroom management skills to the limit when discussing such sensitive issues.

Drawing on over 30 years of teaching these issues, let me help by sharing with you my top ten tips for doing PSHE education right and doing it well:

1. Once you know who is in your PSHE class, speak to pastoral leads so that you are aware of any issues with individual students. This will be easier, of course, if you are teaching PSHE to your own form class.

2. Know your school's safeguarding policy. Know who your designated safeguarding lead is. Know how to report concerns.

3. If possible, be available at the end of class to listen to students who don't wish to speak in front of the class or have something to disclose. However, never promise confidentiality.

4. Introduce a class agreement right from the first session. This should be something you create together with the children and young people, which is referred to every lesson and can be amended as necessary. A class agreement helps to set the expectations to ensure a positive and safe learning environment.

5. Double-check that the topic and your resources are appropriate for the age and ability of your class.

6. Have a variety of activities ready – brainstorming, pair work, small group work, independent work and so on. It's often better if students work with their friends.

7. Always build in time for reflection and feedback. Listen to what students have to say.

8. Try to finish the lesson on a positive. For example, if you have just been discussing coercive and controlling relationships, make sure you wrap up by talking about healthy relationships. For some topics, you might need to let students know where they can get further help and advice. You could have a list of helpful websites signposted in the classroom. Refer to these, and add to them, as necessary.

9. Don't be afraid to tell students that you are not a specialist on a particular subject. It's OK not to be an expert on everything, and if you don't know your dizzle from your skag and the most up-to-date street names for all the other illegal drugs, that's OK. However, do make sure you can direct students to relevant sources of information that they can access themselves.

10. Build in ways to assess the impact of your PSHE sessions: something as simple as 'before' and 'after' questionnaires would do. This will help your future planning and will build your confidence.

In addition, wherever possible, bring in outside expertise – not to replace your role but to complement it. Contributors from police officers to health professionals can all help enrich PSHE taught in schools. Special events, drop-down days, focus days, day trips and visits can all enhance the experience that the children and young people have of these important topics and equip them with valuable life skills which extend beyond the classroom to promote good health and well-being.[1] One of my favourite school trips is a visit to the Houses of Parliament; this is one I would strongly recommend if we want our young people to find their voice and know how to use it! Please note that such events should complement but never replace a regular, timetabled PSHE programme.

Visits and special events might also involve collaborations with other schools in the area. For example, transition days arranged by a secondary school for local primaries can focus on online safety, foreign languages or even public speaking. As head of citizenship and PSHE, I loved organising our annual Model United Nations conference for the Year 6s from our feeder schools. The positive impact on all involved – primary and secondary staff, sixth-form ambassadors, GCSE citizenship studies students and the primary pupils – was huge!

PSHE can be – and needs to be – done well. It's too important not to approach it with the same seriousness as any other aspect of the curriculum and, when you do that, it reveals opportunities for truly memorable educational experiences – the sort you won't get from a pile of vaguely embarrassing handouts.

Now retired from teaching, Pauline Stirling taught for over 30 years; most recently as head of citizenship and PSHE. She is author of Explore PSHE at Key Stage 3. *Passionate about global learning and learning outside the classroom, she is also an ambassador for British Council Schools and Teach SDGs.*

---

1   The British Council has a wealth of free resources, and online and face-to-face opportunities. Some involve collaboration with schools around the globe.

Chapter 11
Going with the Flow

Melanie Gentles

'Is it the end of the lesson yet?'

It's an all-too-common cry, but all the more concerning when you find yourself crying it and you're the teacher.

Let's be honest, the thought of double maths – yes, that's a whole 90 minutes – with the youngest Key Stage 2 children or struggling learners, can fill teacher and students in equal measure with dread. You can throw in as many 'brain breaks' as you dare to keep everyone from flagging too much, concentrating too little or asking to go to the loo too often, but there has to be another way.

Fortunately, there is an approach that can turn 'Is it the end *yet?*' to 'Is it the end *already?*' The answer lies in our understanding of positive psychology and especially in the work of American-Hungarian psychologist (and the man with most commonly mispronounced name in education) Mihaly Csikszentmihalyi.

When you see that shift from counting the minutes, to time passing so quickly you don't even notice, you know you have helped shift the learning from one driven by extrinsic motivation to a deeper, more personal intrinsic one. No longer do we have to bribe/reward/threaten the students with a 'quick run outside if you get to the end of question 10 without World War Three kicking off', and you have created a learning environment that has become infinitely more enjoyable, where self-confidence and important self-management skills are being developed.

The answer is 'flow'.

Csikszentmihalyi coined the term in his seminal book, *Flow: The Psychology of Optimal Experience*, describing it as:

> the state in which people are so involved in an activity that nothing else seems to matter; the experience itself is so enjoyable that people will do it at great cost, for the sheer sake of doing it.[1]

When in the magical state of flow, when we are 'in the zone', not only do we enjoy a heightened sense of focus with the improved learning outcomes that brings, but flow can make us happier too. Learning and happiness can go hand in hand. Given that it's the dream of all educators to have a classroom full of happy, focused learners – especially for double maths – how do we set about cultivating this powerful sense of engagement within the children we teach?

The starting point for achieving this educational nirvana is to understand that we are more likely to experience flow when we are employing our primary character strengths. Character strength is one of the major topics in positive psychology. It involves exploring the way that identifying and building on our strengths opens us to personal growth and development. An important role for any teacher in their classroom is that of 'strength spotting' – recognising and identifying the strengths in your students. Armed with this knowledge, you are better able to tailor tasks which build on an individual's strengths rather than push down on their weaknesses.

Strength spotting by the teacher is one thing, but 'strength accepting' on the part of the students is another. In a time where students seem to face constant competition and comparisons both online and in the real world, it is important that they know their strengths and accept that 'yes, this is something I'm a bit handy at!' Self-efficacy is the goal here – 'I can do things, I can solve things, I can overcome things, I can help myself'.

---

1   Mihaly Csikszentmihalyi, *Flow: The Psychology of Optimal Experience* (New York: Harper and Row, 1990), p. 4.

Highlighting and celebrating (not rewarding[2]) what a student does well builds on this important sense of self-efficacy, and it is something that needs to be built into the classroom rules and expectations from day one. In this way you create a classroom culture of kindness, empathy, gratitude and risk-taking; one in which we all work hard to be the best version of ourselves.

Other attributes of such a positive learning environment include the fostering of children's curiosity by asking questions rather than simply providing answers, and discussing their thinking and methods with them rather than simply focusing on whether an answer is right or wrong.

Any task at hand must also have clear learning goals; these help motivate the students, provide a sequential structure for them to work towards and allow them to assess progress along the way. This sense of the student moving towards a goal also means that feedback is relevant and useful, whether that is the immediate feedback from the teacher or the sort of personal feedback derived from asking the three important metacognitive questions: what am I doing? How am I doing? How did I do?

In terms of the nature of the tasks you set, note that students welcome tasks that challenge them, but that are still achievable. Setting stretch goals, and allowing students to set them for themselves, fosters a sense of accomplishment and, as you continue adapting the tasks to their ever-increasing levels of attainment, you will start to see an upward spiral of positive emotions – 'If I can do this, what else can I do?'

The sweet spot you are aiming for is where a student's perceived skill and the perceived size of the challenge are nicely balanced. When this is achieved, the student is confident that the task is doable, even though they do not yet know *how* they will do it.

As you plan your lessons, think about an approach to differentiation that values the different ways that students approach learning so they have choices to make, as well as any specific needs they may have. Taking the time to source additional resources and aids will pay dividends in the lesson because when you give students a choice, this also contributes to the

---

2   A reward is a form of extrinsic motivation, one that may have short-term gains but can be detrimental in the longer term.

flow state, even if they end up choosing what you would have chosen for them anyway. It's the sense they have of being in control that is important.

We know that flow is a vital part of having intrinsically motivated, happy learners. Sometimes it happens without us even thinking about it. You know that lesson where you just wish someone had been observing because you – and the class – absolutely nailed it? That was flow.

It might appear like magic but, as I have shown, you can work to create the conditions where it will appear on command and turn 'Is it time?' to 'Is that the time?' much more often.

Melanie Gentles is a teacher, school leader and mental health lead based in London. Studying for a master's degree in applied positive psychology has set her on a new journey within education and sparked a passion for sharing how evidence-based positive psychology interventions support the well-being of schools, staff and pupils.

Chapter 12

Finding Your Storytelling Voice

Chris Connaughton

That's the first time all term that Katie has said any-thing to the group.

Year 4 teacher

Once upon a time, there was a storyteller who travelled the length and breadth of the kingdom, weaving magical stories for children of all ages. For 25 years he journeyed, sharing and acting stories as he went, creating and hearing even more. The storyteller learned many things on his travels, but one stood out beyond all the others. We don't just like stories. We *need* them to survive. (I know this because I am that itinerant storyteller.)

We need stories in order to evolve as individuals and to develop as families, and it is stories that hold a society together. After all, when a society starts telling different stories, the cracks soon start to appear. From the Big Bad Wolf to Beowulf, soap opera to high opera, an amusing tale told by our favourite comedian to the latest joke to go around the office, we all thrive on and are thrilled by a good story.

It starts in early childhood, of course. At home or in the classroom, the stories we share with children are always more than simple tales of curious people doing interesting things. They serve to quieten fears, to warn of dangers, to develop language and to strengthen parental bonds. And they do so by filling us with wide-eyed wonder or hysterical delight. The very best stories do all of these things simultaneously, and even a half-decent yarn will manage at least a couple of them before we get to 'happily ever after'. Stories teach us things about the world, but they also offer up deeper meanings about ourselves. I read biographies and history books to learn about others, but I read novels to learn about myself.

So I'd like to focus on the way that telling stories can impact our children as they begin to experiment with their own voice and the many different ways that they have of expressing themselves. But I'm also going to suggest that the very act of storytelling can help us – parents and teachers – to discover and speak in our own voice too.

Even when we know the importance of story, even when we accept that it can be an incredibly powerful tool in education, many of us remain tongue-tied. In the classroom or presenting an assembly – especially presenting an assembly – many teachers feel uncertain, lacking confidence in their skills as storytellers. Sadly, this leads many of us to shy away from such a vital, valuable activity. We don't tell stories for fear of the voice that comes out.

Many actors speak of being shy and reserved as children. I have even heard acting being described as the 'shy person's revenge'. Yet with someone else's lines to say or with a character to hide behind, those nerves magically disappear.

It's not easy (even for a seasoned professional performer such as myself!), but the following exercises might help. I share them with you as a starting point for you to find your own route towards reading and performing, or even making up your own stories, and to help you on the journey to finding your voice.

Picture the scene. There is a young drama student and he is trying to get his tongue around the name 'Constantin Stanislavski'. This man, the student is being told, was a theatre director; one of the best ever. And he was Russian. 'What made him great?' the student asks. Two key elements, he is told, which many still think of as the Stanislavski method for acting.

The 'magic if' was the first one I was told about (for I was that drama student). You may already be familiar with this idea but not know where it came from. It entails asking ourselves the question 'What if it were me in this situation?' What would I think? What would I feel? And then, based on my answers, what would I do?

Try it. Imagine that you wake up one day after a short nap and there is a great big daddy bear staring down at you as you wake up. What would you think, feel, do?

Try it again. You come home one day after a trip out with the family and not only do you find a young blonde girl asleep in your bed and one of your kitchen chairs in pieces, but some of your porridge is missing. Again, what would you think, feel, do next?

Try another. You arrive home really, really excited, beside yourself, fit to burst. You know you were supposed to get money for the cow you had sold but you've got something much better – magic beans! How are you thinking, feeling and acting now? How are you thinking, feeling and acting once your mum has shouted at you and sent you to bed for being so gullible?

Let's try one more. What would you say to yourself if you knew you had made a terrible mistake because, even though your dad, the woodcutter, had told you not to, you had talked to that wolf?

To find your storytelling voice, simply use your answers to these questions to inform how you might tell your own version of the story. And it's not just to help with your own storytelling voice, of course. The 'magic if' can open up all kinds of conversations in class too. You can use the context of a story to develop important skills like oracy and emotional literacy, as well as to help your students expand their vocabulary. For example, using that same 'magic if' technique, you can follow up a story session with these conversation starters:

- What would you feel like if you were lost in a deep, dark forest?

- If you were given three wishes by a wood fairy, what would you wish for?

- If you really did find a wolf hiding in your granny's pyjamas, what would you think? And what would you say?

- If the birds really did eat all the crumbs and you couldn't find the path home, how would you feel?

Of course, despite how vivid an imagination many children display, they just don't know what it's really like to climb a beanstalk, meet cobbling elves or find a wolf where their grandma should be. This means you might get some blank looks.

Stanislavski suggested that we can all tap into our emotion memory; that is to say, the memory of the feelings of all the emotions we have ever experienced. We can use these memories to help us get past the 'I haven't done those things so I don't know how I would react' scenario. For example, saying to a class, 'Hands up who's come face to face with a bear' or 'Hands up who's been trapped in a tower' or 'Hands up if you've ever had a wolf blow your house down' might not get you very far. On the other paw, asking, 'Who's been scared before?' will never fail to result in a sea of eagerly waving hands. That sea of hands, by the way, should include your own. This way you are showing to the children that it's alright to have felt this way, and that they are not alone in their experience and that you are onside with them.

Once you have their attention and have thanked them for their honesty (stories are also about inclusion, safety, reassurance and some of your children might not get much of these things outside the classroom so it needs to be acknowledged when you see it) go for a second question: 'Hands up if you've ever felt lonely or upset about something?' is a good one. Again, ensure that you put your own hand up to encourage the class and add something like, 'That's lots of you again. Thank you. But don't worry if you haven't felt that.' Again, you are prioritising safety and inclusion.

Next you might ask my favourite question: 'Now, who can remember feeling really excited about something that was going to happen?' You see their eyes light up and grins growing on their faces as their hands shoot up. This is emotion memory in action. The children are actually remembering what it was like and experiencing it again, in that moment. Remember to let your own eyes light up too and to smile at them, engaging eye contact to draw them all in.

Having had a feeling is one thing. Knowing what the feeling feels like is something else. Next you can ask questions like 'Who can tell us what it feels like to be sad or upset, scared or happy?' Do allow the children time to respond fully here. I know I'm often guilty of jumping in and helping them answer, filling in their response in my own way, but I really shouldn't. This is *their* answer, and searching for the best way to express it is an important part of developing conversational skills. Let it come from them. Be mindful of the cathartic moment that might be playing out before your eyes and ears, and take it seriously. Make sure you also give different children opportunities to speak. Many may never get the chance to voice an opinion, or even know what one is, and now is their time. Remember to keep the whole process inclusive, reassuring and safe, and use the world of the story and the context of the characters to help with this.

Once we have established that, although never having been up a beanstalk, we have all felt the feelings that Jack might have been experiencing – his mother's angry words ringing in his ears – it's time to push them a bit further for a description and develop language that can be used in their own stories.

Asking questions like 'What happens in your tummy if you're excited?' or 'What does your heart do if something makes you jump?' will generate some great ideas about feelings and emotions and the fabulous language that comes with them. Note that we are still talking fairy tales and long ago and far away, but the students are actually talking about *themselves*. It has become personal and now they have more ownership of the story.

I had a feeling Stanislavski was on to something. It turns out that there was another important bit in his method: that of building a character.

To avoid getting bogged down in the ego and super-objectives and through-lines of emotions, I created the Walking, Actions, Voice and Emotions (WAVE) game along with a teacher colleague and consultant, Shonette Bason. For young children, character building is all about faces, movements and relationships with other characters, and so WAVE is a simple and effective tool for helping children to describe a character in detail. So, for example, how might a character move around a space? What gestures might they display? What might they say and how might they say it? And what emotions might they portray through their words, actions and even the look on their face?

By breaking down a character, or a section of story you want the children to retell, into these four elements, I have found that even reluctant speakers have discovered ways to speak and perform as a variety of characters. For example, either on the spot or moving around, I like to get the group walking, in character, followed by doing an action they think is appropriate to the character's feelings. Next I ask them to show an emotion on their face before adding a voice right at the end. Why leave the voice until last? Because, by then, they have all the other elements to support them, helping them to find a word or a simple sentence with more confidence. I have found that many children have a far better grasp of complex ideas, language and storylines than we often give them credit for. So let's trust them with exciting new plot structures and with fantastic, fabulous, different words.

Notice I say 'different', not 'difficult' or 'challenging'. Encountering new language, vocabulary and ideas needs to be an adventure for children, not something dangerous. Language should hold out a promise, not a threat. If we focus only on spelling and pronunciation and looking clever and using the words that will most impress the inspector, we turn new language from a key to a cage.

As I found in my journey from drama student to storyteller, when we summon our own confidence to tell a story, we encourage children to be confident too. With that new-found confidence they too will learn to speak, to invent, to imagine, and to make their voice heard though the stories they tell.

Chris Connaughton is an actor, storyteller and writer for children who tours his work throughout schools in the UK. He has written plays for Theatre Hullabaloo and a wide variety of stories and novels. His latest book, Hospital by the Hill, which deals with childhood bereavement, includes a foreword specially written by Prince Harry.

Chapter 13

Curious Learners in Creative Ways

Sarah Hepworth

The more time I have spent in teaching and school leadership, the more I find myself both engaged with the research on how to bring the best out of children, and in honest reflection about what works for me. I have always thrived on having a class where children ask questions and actively become involved in their own learning, but I have not thought about how I achieve this; that is, until now. Here, then, are my suggestions for helping children be curious, excited and motivated about learning inside and outside of the classroom.

Like many, I'm sure, I have taught in classrooms where role play areas were an essential part of our environment. I have created numerous book corners in my classrooms to encourage the love of reading,[1] and have crafted displays that I hoped would inspire learners and help with their depth of understanding. This is all well and good, but one thing I hadn't done was work in a school with a focus on what we might call 'immersive learning'. In 2021, however, in response to the COVID-19 pandemic, our children's missed learning and the national lockdowns (and 'knowing more of the same, but quicker' was not going to cut it) my school made the decision to pursue this approach to teaching and learning. The hope was that by immersing children in their learning, we would deepen their understand-

---

1   My work as a group leader for the Open University and UK Literacy Association teachers' reading groups makes me now realise that a reading culture is so much more than this alone.

ing, improve engagement, develop them as questioners and also keep them motivated.

The decision we took meant we needed to have a serious think about how to develop curious learners in creative ways. My studies for the National Professional Qualification for Senior Leaders helped me understand that learning should spark curiosity and fuel children's excitement. Sir Ken Robinson defines creativity as 'the process of having original ideas that have value' whilst also highlighting that imagination is essential in creating creativity,[2] which is why I love developing a curriculum with books, storytelling, oracy and curiosity at its heart. By immersing children in a book or a topic, we spark their natural interest, but by bringing these books alive, we create curious and excited learners who strive to learn beyond the classroom.

To create curious learners, you have to give them something to be genuinely curious about. This is where our curiosity cases came in, adapted from the idea of the curiosity cubes used in early years. In the cubes, children discover clues to a book or a topic and then have the time to explore the relevant and contextual knowledge that will deepen their engagement; something that will also encourage children to ask not only more but better questions. And children who ask in-depth questions become great learners.

Old suitcases are perfect for creating curiosity cases and everyone, staff included, was eager to touch and explore the items they found inside – objects found in resource cupboards, picked up cheap at car boot sales or even made specifically for the job. The magician's trick of concealment followed by the slow reveal was wonderful for generating excitement and curiosity, much more so than simply displaying the items on a table. Curiosity cases are not a new concept, but I do wish I had used them earlier in my career.[3]

---

2   MindShift, Ken Robinson: Creativity is in everything, especially teaching, *KQED* (22 April 2015). Available at: https://www.kqed.org/mindshift/40217/sir-ken-robinson-creativity-is-in-everything-especially-teaching..

3   Indeed, cabinets of curiosity have been around for centuries. For more on this, see Matthew McFall, *The Little Book of Awe and Wonder: A Cabinet of Curiosities* (Carmarthen: Independent Thinking Press, 2018).

One of the reasons they are so successful links to something Daniel Willingham has pointed out: that problem solving and curiosity actually bring pleasure to a learner in a way that simply knowing an answer fails to do.[4] The curiosity cases do just that. They bring pleasure by encouraging problem solving, letting questioning flourish and igniting curiosity. What's more, they are versatile, easy (and cheap) to create and are a wonderful start to creating an immersive environment for a topic. But suitcases full of curious artefacts are just the start.

In Year 4 we were looking at the topic of explorers. Taking one book – *The Explorer* by Katherine Rundell[5] – as our inspiration, we transformed our shared area into a rainforest, with creatures 'wandering' from there into classrooms to pique the children's interest; we launched the topic with a Forest School survival day (which both staff and children still talk about); we discussed and debated hot topics such as the key things we all need in order to survive, whether some areas should be left untouched and the impact of exploring on the world; and we brought countries to life, exploring them through Google Earth, documentaries, diaries, sharing our own experiences and much more.

We underpinned all of this by looking closely at what knowledge was needed, what knowledge and skills the children wanted to develop and what the best sequence was for exploring these things, and we ensured that their knowledge and understanding accumulated over the term. In this way, children learned and made connections at a far deeper level; they were actively asking questions which were relevant and deeply thought out, and they were independently continuing their research beyond the classrooms. They also helped fuel each other's interest and excitement, bringing in books to share top facts and recommending documentaries they had seen.

The development of questioning skills was also a key focus for us and my research had shown me the importance of modelling to children how to ask higher order questions – something that dovetailed nicely with our immersive work and the opportunities it threw up to create deeper thinkers. Seeing children as a species who seek challenge and questions means

---

4   Daniel Willingham, *Why Don't Students Like School?* (San Francisco, CA: Jossey-Bass, 2010).

5   Katherine Rundell, *The Explorer* (London: Bloomsbury, 2017).

we need to excite them, pique their interest and get them asking great questions to drive their learning deeper.[6]

As a Forest School leader, I would also like to point out the many benefits of taking immersive learning outside. If we are looking for at least one positive from the pandemic, it is that it has encouraged more schools and practitioners to get outside. Natural environments offer so many great opportunities for our learners. For some, the tactile environment helps them literally grasp the learning far more quickly and deeply; for others, the freedom of the outdoors can alleviate classroom anxieties; and, for all, the world beyond the classroom can really open their imaginations to the full.[7]

In another unit we transformed our shared area into a *Fantastic Beasts* environment where mysterious animal eggs, skin samples from interesting creatures and old diaries from Hogwarts could be found in our curiosity case; something we put in the middle of our 'Magizoologist's Study'. During this term we also focused on another key area in our pursuit of creative, curious leaners – developing autonomy through creativity.

Children investigated dragon eggs, created their own clay-potted Mandrakes and explored how authors and creators develop other hybrid or unique characters, before then choosing the direction their own creature creations would take and, importantly, how they wanted to share what they had learned. By giving them ownership as learners, I have seen their motivation and pride increase through their eagerness to share their masterpieces and have also witnessed greater levels of reflection and independence as they strive for their best.

My research into the teaching of vocabulary had taught me that we need to make our environments rich and that a fun and multi-sensory approach works to activate as many beneficial connections in their brains as possible. For example, when teaching a word, we play with the language and the way it sounds – we clap, sing and bellow, as well as looking at the word represented in pictures and activating it in our minds with drama and actions. That is all before we ever write the word.

---

6   Mary Myatt, *The Curriculum: Gallimaufry to Coherence* (Woodbridge: John Catt Educational, 2018).

7   For more on taking your learning outside, see Juliet Robertson, *Dirty Teaching: A Beginner's Guide to Learning Outdoors* (Carmarthen: Independent Thinking Press, 2014).

We can apply this research across all areas of the curriculum in order to bring learning to life. Such 'pre-teaching' allows us to develop a deeper understanding of key Tier 2 and Tier 3 words prior to teaching the lessons, and this pre-exposure helps create confident learners who are able to use prior learning, build upon it and then deepen it. It also improves the quality of the questions they ask, ensuring they are more closely linked to the topic content and richer – less generic – too.

As I write this, we are now a year down the line and I can honestly say that our aim to instil curiosity, motivation and questioning has not only been achieved for our children but for our staff too. In order to create these immersive opportunities and this depth of learning, teachers make the most significant difference when they are experts. By immersing them in rich topics, deepening their knowledge and working with them to foster a creative and exciting curriculum, they go on to nurture curious learners. Autonomy in this is as vital for the staff as it is for the children, and it is crucial to allow staff to take the learning in a direction that excites them. After all, if the staff aren't excited to deliver it, the children won't be excited to explore. When everyone is excited to learn together, that's when we see the true lightbulb moments and you know you have helped create confident, creative, curious learners.

In over 10 years in education, Sarah Hepworth has taught across all phases, either with her own classes or through coaching and mentoring. She has presented to head teachers, presented at Educating Northants and delivered training for the 5 Wells Development Centre. She is also an Open University/ UK Literacy Association reading leader and newly designated evidence lead in education for Derby Research School.

Chapter 14

Understanding Schemata in Five Quotes

Nick Stewart

Schemata are nothing new. We have known since the Ancient Greeks and the idea of 'memory palaces' that new learning works best when we hook it into existing knowledge. And they are nothing to be scared of either. By understanding what they are and how they work, we can plan lessons that work with, not against, the way we all learn best.

One

People use schemata (the plural of schema) to categorize objects and events based on common elements and characteristics and thus interpret and predict the world.[1]

The simple way I regard schemata is to think of them as the way the brain organises new material by linking new experiences with existing memories and previously learned experiences that are already present in the memory.[2]

---

1   Katja Michalak, Schema, *Encyclopædia Britannica* (2019). Available at: https://www.britannica.com/science/schema-cognitive.

2   For more on this, see John Medina, Schema [video], *YouTube* (2008). Available at: https://www.youtube.com/watch?v=mzbRpMlEHzM&t=112s.

How are you specifically linking new knowledge to existing knowledge in your lessons?

Two

When students are able to relate to the learning, they are better able to explore content and mentally engage in rigorous, meaningful thought.[3]

I try to build upon a student's schemata by asking questions when introducing a new topic or getting them to think and discuss a related topic. For example, I have taught how to calculate the area under a curved graph to two high-ability classes: with the first class, I dived straight in and the class struggled to understand and remember the concept; with the second class, armed with a better understanding of the role of schemata in learning, I started with questions that encouraged students to first look more widely at calculating the area of shapes, including rectangles, triangles and trapeziums. I knew they had done this previously in the curriculum. After a few questions, and a whole-class discussion to ensure all students could identify the parallel sides in a trapezium, I then displayed a curved graph: the new element that I wanted them to understand.

After starting with, 'What is the connection between our starter and this graph?', the class finally arrived at the idea of approximating the curve to a trapezium. It was then relatively easy for them to spot that, instead of drawing one big trapezium, it would be better to split the area into three or four separate shapes. They identified that the best way was to use a mixture of triangles and trapeziums. The rest of the lesson was spent with them working through similar questions with minimal input from me.

How are you planning to introduce new topics by having (at least) a starter on a related topic that the students are already familiar with?

---

3   Pennsylvania Department of Education, Activating student schema (2021). Available at: http://pdcenter.pdesas.org/CourseRendering/CourseContent/Render/236070195168027248188003114051035160213163237114.

Three

Instructors must help students develop the appropriate new schemata. It has been additionally beneficial when I have assisted students with the identification of keywords and clarification of meaning.[4]

What can be really helpful is for the teacher to develop 'hooks' for students that can be reinforced and built upon by future revisits, both to the topic and to the hooks again. I have started to alter my teaching to ensure that students become familiar with concepts which I hook onto new keywords and short phrases or symbols. Like the tip of an iceberg, by successfully re-accessing the hook, the learning below the surface comes back to mind, without having to review the entire iceberg each time.

What keywords and hooks can you introduce and review regularly to help fix the wider topic into their long-term memory?

Four

Although initial schema acquisition entails working memory resources, use of schemata becomes automated with sufficient practice to require minimal working memory resources.[5]

It is important to cover new content at a slower pace and with regular review, not only to ensure students understand the new material as they work through it, but also to lay down firm foundations in their long-term memory for later retrieval. By encouraging students to identify and use pre-existing schemata – or help them build new ones – they will be able to access the knowledge in their long-term memory and ease the pressure on their working memory.

----

4   Jeffrey Czarnec and Michelle G. Hill, Schemata and instructional strategies, *The EvoLLLution* (2018). Available at: https://evolllution.com/programming/teaching-and-learning/schemata-and-instructional-strategies/.

5   Czarnec and Hill, Schemata and instructional strategies.

Note that it is important to chunk the new material into coherent and clear component parts. As students continue to build schema as they become more expert at a topic, they are able to call on more schemata. This works best when it is systematically organised in a hierarchical fashion. By being able to call on these effectively stored schemata, they need to use less working memory than the novice.

Rosenshine describes how effective teachers present 'small amounts of new material at one time' to ensure that each point is mastered and understood, then checked and retaught if necessary, before moving on.[6] Misconceptions can occur, he suggests, when a student's prior knowledge is weak or faulty and they create logical but incorrect connections.

How fast are you moving from prior to new knowledge, and how are you checking for any deficiencies in prior understanding and putting it right before you move on?

Five

Whenever an instructional treatment encourages students to replace an existing, effective learning strategy with a dissimilar alternative, learning is depressed.[7]

Looking specifically at the teaching of maths, but with wider implications for all teachers, researcher Richard Clark suggests there are two different outcomes when we plan activities in a lesson. A task could be either 'mathemagenic', which promotes – literally 'gives birth to' – learning, or 'mathemathantic', which actually kills learning. This latter type of task achieves this dubious result primarily by mismatching a strategy with the levels of competency of the learner.

---

6   Barak Rosenshine, Principles of instruction: research-based strategies that all teachers should know, *American Educator* 36(1) (2012): 12. Available at: https://eric.ed.gov/?id=EJ971753.

7   Richard Clark, When teaching kills learning (1989), cited in Becton Loveless, A complete guide to schema theory and its role in education, *Education Corner* (12 April 2022). Available at: https://www.educationcorner.com/schema-theory/.

It is important to remember that a task that might be mathemagenic at the beginning of a topic may end up mathemathantic later, as the learner acquires a greater understanding of the topic and as their schema develops. We need, then, to match our tasks with the individual learner's growth with a view to 'leaving them to it' a whole lot more as their proficiency increases.

What are you doing to ensure your teaching isn't getting in the way of their learning? How are you matching the tasks you set to their levels of competency and making sure nothing you are doing is, despite your best intentions, killing their learning?

*

Nick Stewart is a secondary school maths teacher who has been teaching for over a decade. For the first 7 years he was at a school in Hertfordshire and has since moved to West Devon. He has a master's degree in education, which was a good qualification to gain, but his real interest in improving his teaching and improving the learning of his students came from joining Twitter.

Part III

Tiny Voices Talk About Inclusion

I was at school a long time ago. It was after the use of the cane had been banned, but teachers resorted to other odd and sometimes cruel measures of behaviour management and, in my opinion, had little tolerance for anything but the 'norm'.

When I was 7, I was in a class with three boys – MS, ST and MF – all of whom I remember vividly. MS was obsessed with nature and learning about the world around him. We were friends with his family outside of school and he would usually be found down the end of the garden, making friends with the bugs. He was always being told off for not paying attention to lessons, instead drawing diagrams of animals. ST could not sit still. He was always in trouble for 'fidgeting' and not listening. MF was always in trouble for swearing and saying inappropriate things. (Yes, there was a great deal of 'always' back then.) And me, well, I spent most of that year being thrown up the stairs to the head teacher's room – sometimes quite literally. You can probably guess why: talking too much.

Looking back, with my teacher lenses on, I wonder now if MS was potentially on the autistic spectrum, if ST had attention deficit hyperactivity disorder (ADHD) and MF had Tourette's. I may be completely wrong, but I do wonder. What I do know is that they were made to eat soap or drink washing up liquid most days. I am not sure if the teacher thought that this was a way to cleanse them and normalise them. There was no desire on the teacher's part to understand the children in her class or help them, and difference was punished.

I think that is one of the reasons why I believe it is so important to embrace the uniqueness of every child in my class and find out what they need. I don't just want to treat every child equally; I want to treat them equitably. I love this quote from Naheed Dosani on Twitter: '#Equality is giving everyone a shoe. #Equity is giving everyone a shoe that fits.'[1]

I hope that the chapters in this section will give you a greater understanding of what to consider regarding inclusion in your classroom and school – special needs and disabilities, family circumstances, heritage, culture, gender, sexuality and so much more.

I know that MS, ST and MF's school experiences would be entirely different if they were at school today, but I do think that we still have a long way to go in order to ensure that every child is celebrated in classrooms around the world. Celebrated for being the unique and wonderful young people they are.

1   Naheed Dosani (@NaheedD), Twitter post (3 April 2014, 11.23 p.m.). Available at: https://twitter.com/naheedd/status/451847459242012672.

Chapter 15

Nine Reasons to Love Your SENCO

Penny Whelan

I'm in love. I didn't plan for it to happen or even imagine it would, but now it has, I can honestly say I'm head over heels. It's not easy but it's worth it. Yes, becoming a special educational needs coordinator (SENCO) was one of the best things ever to happen to me.

In case you don't yet share my passion for the role of school SEN and/or disabilities coordinator, here are nine reasons why you should love your SENCO as much as I love being one.

1. SENCOs are on your side

SENCOs work with teachers to support children. That's what they are for. They are fully aware of the amazing work you are doing with your class, and the reason they want to work with you – and have to ask you to complete the relevant SEN paperwork – is because you know the children better than anyone else. They really want, need and value your input.

2. SENCOs understand what you're facing

SENCOs know how hard teaching children with SEN can be when you have so many other children to look after in your class. But they also know that what you do with that SEN child to support them is superb and makes a real difference. They know your workload is never ending and they hate adding to it, really they do, but sometimes they unavoidably have to ask for things.

3. SENCOs want the best for the children

Whether your SENCO chose that role or had it thrust upon them, they are still a teacher and an educator like you. And they want what you want – what's best for the children. If they are asking you to do something or are arranging interventions or whatever is needed, they are doing it with the best interests of the child at heart.

4. SENCOs don't have all the answers

Think of a SENCO as a specialist who doesn't know everything. Yes, they have to take the National Award for SENCOs (NASENCO), which provides a degree of important training, but they aren't complete experts in specific conditions that present as special needs. They can't diagnose different difficulties and, when you talk to them about a child, they might not know what the issue is. However, what they will do is their absolute best to find out what that child needs, how to support them as much as possible and how you can all work together to achieve this.

5. SENCOs struggle with their workload just as much as you do

A SENCO has *a lot* of paperwork to complete. Every referral takes pages of information, and an education, health and care plan is a seriously extensive document which has to prove that you have tried a variety of different methods to support a child, that you have involved many outside agencies and that the child needs significantly more support than the vast majority of their peers. That's a lot of evidence to fit in a document. There will be days when your SENCO feels completely overwhelmed by their 'to do' list and worries that they aren't doing as much as they feel they should be.

6. SENCOs want you to speak to them about the children

No matter how busy a SENCO is, they always want you to talk to them about the children in your class and any concerns or questions you may have. No one knows the children like you do, apart from their parents, so your input is genuinely valuable. If you have concerns over a child's needs, they really do need to know about it. That way, you can work together to identify what should be happening next.

7. There are always people there to support your SENCO

SENCOs are not alone. In the same way you may be hooked into a subject specialism or year-group network, there are always ways that SENCOs can connect with other SENCOs. Most local authorities have a SENCO network they can join, not to mention tapping into shared communities such as Twitter. Encourage them to be part of these networks and take an interest when they are.

8. The local authority has a tough job too

Just because your SENCO is the route to get support from your local authority or other outside agency, it still might take a while, so please be patient. The local authority works incredibly hard to support a huge number of pupils, families and schools, and so we all need to work together to do what's best for the children. It's a team effort – make sure you're on board.

9. A SENCO is a human being

Your SENCO is mortal and has as much chance of getting all their jobs done in one day as you do. Encourage them to get any help they might need, including admin support, and be on their side and supportive in their conversations with the head or senior leadership team. If they are a class teacher as well as SENCO, please be patient as they juggle their different roles and do their very best to support you and the pupils.

*

Developing a great working relationship with your SENCO really can make a difference to a child's life and, for us SENCOs, it's such a privileged position to be in. Love your SENCO and you'll help them to love their role as much as I do.

Penny Whelan is a primary assistant head teacher and SENCO. She has a bachelor's degree in psychology and a Postgraduate Certificate in Education. Penny works part time and is also English as an additional language coordinator, a specialist leader in education, a coach and the operations manager for the Schools Linking Network in her local authority. She is passionate about special educational needs and disabilities, inclusion, community and diversity.

Chapter 16
Fabulous Forces Families

Shelly Cozens

My children have not had the childhood that I had. Growing up, I lived in the same house from the age of 4 until I left for university at 18. I had the same group of friends and together we attended the village primary, local secondary and, later, sixth form. Yes, there were some tricky 'growing up' moments, but what I had remained stable and familiar. My three children are having a vastly different childhood. Why? Because as well as being a mother and a teacher, I am also a military wife.

In the 12 years I have been with my husband, he has been away on active service eight times, the longest deployment being 8 long months. Twice we have had the gruelling heartbreak of cancelled homecomings. Our children are aged between 5 and 16. This life is tough for me. It is even harder for them.

If you want a case study in resilience, look at the children of forces families like mine. In their short lives they have experienced moves to various parts of the country, made new friends as often as they have had to say goodbye to old ones thanks to fresh military postings and, most heartbreakingly, had to say goodbye to their own daddy countless times, sometimes for months on end, knowing in that unspoken way that he is going somewhere dangerous. Military children experience a unique lifestyle that shapes the young people they become, but this unique childhood means they often need extra-special support at school.

In August 2020 I was asked to speak at the #BrewEdFindYourVoice event, which went out live on Twitter. I wanted to raise awareness about this wonderful group of children, a group that is often overlooked. For those living near military bases, there is often support on hand. But what about those who are miles away from such help? Who is making sure they are OK? Who has the well-being and welfare of these families in their sights?

While the advice I could give would fill an entire book, here are some top tips that I know will help you help this exceptional group of children, starting with your first challenge – finding out who the military children are in your school. If you draw a blank with your school records, then your annual census data is a good starting place. If and when you find you have service children in your school, then please tread carefully. Not all families want their children to be singled out or made to feel different in any way. I have always been grateful for any help and support on offer for my children, but experience has taught me that not all families feel the same way.

The next port of call is to check out the work of Service Children in State Schools.[1] Led by the National Executive Advisory Committee, its aim is to provide advice and support to schools. If you are in Wales, then Supporting Service Children in Education Wales offers similar support,[2] as does Forces Children's Education in Scotland.[3]

As you do your research, another resource that I know teachers find invaluable, wherever they are based, is the free Thriving Lives Toolkit.[4] Through a process of reflective practice and continuing professional development, the toolkit encourages schools to consider how they can support forces children to succeed in education. These whole-school approaches can transform the lives of a largely invisible minority of forces children who are living away from regular bases.

School-wide approaches are important, of course, but what you do in your classroom counts too. I highly recommend the resources packs on offer from the charity Little Troopers, which cater for both primary and secondary students and are, again, free.[5]

---

1   See https://www.sciss.org.uk.
2   See https://www.sscecymru.co.uk/.
3   See https://forceschildrenseducation.org.uk/.
4   See https://www.scipalliance.org/thriving-lives-toolkit.
5   See https://www.littletroopers.net/.

You should always contact the families federations of the respective service too; they can offer you specific advice for supporting your young people. Note that this is where your service pupil premium funding can come into play, so make sure you ringfence it accordingly, not just lump the £310 that is available annually (at the time of writing) for forces children into the general pupil premium pot. Parents can and do – and should – ask where the funding is being spent, and it is another piece of information that needs to be readily available on your school website.

Of course, any attempt to support the learning outcomes of forces children must consider the enormity of the emotional rollercoaster they are on. Even before their parent leaves on deployment, the strains of the heightened emotions involved for everyone start to show. Sadness, fear and even anger may simmer up in the classroom, becoming more intense as the day of departure approaches, after which a new routine can settle into place, for a while anyway.

Then there are the equally heightened but different emotions connected to the homecoming. The return of the parent or carer sees a new dynamic for the household, and not always an easy one. You don't just leave a war zone behind. Be sensitive to this and recognise, for example, that authorising a term-time holiday for them to all address a prolonged separation is more important than your attendance data. Not every head teacher may agree with this statement, but as someone who has been on the receiving end of such kindness, please believe me when I say that it can make an enormous difference to a family's emotional well-being.

So, there we have it – a snapshot of how to start supporting forces children. There is a wealth of information out there, and now you know where to start. I would urge you to do some further investigation in your setting to ensure that inclusive education takes on a whole new dimension. Life can be tough for forces children. How will you make a difference to that child in your class who, like my children, are facing another year without one parent?

Shelly Cozens is an English teacher and head of careers and cultural capital, based in the south-west of England. As an experienced teacher, mother of three and wife of a serving member of the armed forces, she offers a personal perspective on how schools can support forces children in education.

Chapter 17

What Letter Are You?

Jared Cawley

I decided to wear a Progress Pride flag pin on my school lanyard. It was the first time I had dared to do this. That day, a boy in my class sees it, puts his pen down, stands up and approaches my desk.

Student: Mr. Cawley …

Me: Yes?

Student: Is that the LGBTQ+ flag on your badge?

Me: Yes, it is.

Student: I thought I recognised it. Does that mean you're LGBTQ+?

Me: Yes, it does.

Student: So, what letter are you?

Me: I'm part of the 'G' community. G stands for 'gay'.

Student: Ah, OK. My uncle is part of the 'G' community too.

He returns to his table and gets on with his work.

Moments like this are probably happening up and down the country and show one way in which a tiny interaction can have a huge impact. Making your school or classroom lesbian, gay, bisexual, transgender and queer plus

(LGBTQ+) friendly must begin with small, deliberate steps. We must acknowledge that this will not happen overnight. But, with thoughtful planning and an open mind, a school can create a culture of inclusivity for everyone.

Why, though, if you are not a member of the LGBTQ+ community should this concern you? Why is it important to be an LGBTQ+ ally?

All of us have the same hopes and expectations in our place of work. We all want to be seen, to be heard, to feel like we belong and to feel that we are safe to be ourselves. The thing is, as a member of the LGBTQ+ community, I am used to being silenced, to feeling invisible, to feeling unsafe. Isolation and vigilance are a large part of my working life.[1] Schools are, after all, places where heterosexuality and heteronormativity are privileged and the norm. Just look at your story books. Working life for people like me requires some careful navigation.

If you are not straight, you learn to be careful. If you are straight, you may not know what it's like to be the victim of abuse and discrimination for just expressing who you are. You won't know what it's like to be on the receiving end of the many names there are for a queer person like me. You won't have been beaten up in the street, like I was, for holding hands with the person you love. You won't have had to confront the people who do this and who justify their actions as entirely acceptable and legitimate. I always wonder, would these attacks have happened if these people had been given an education that normalised LGBTQ+ lives?

Which brings me to one of my most important points. As educators, we all have a responsibility – and a legal obligation[2] – to sustain and promote a school culture that welcomes diversity, supports equality and actively challenges any behaviours that may jeopardise equity for all. Note too that if you are a teacher or school leader who identifies as heterosexual, or is not part of a minority group, you are less likely to notice the exclusion or the

---

1   Tania Ferfolja and Efty Stavrou, Workplace experiences of Australian lesbian and gay teachers: findings from a national survey, *Canadian Journal of Educational Administration and Policy* 173 (2015): 113–138. Available at: https://files.eric. ed.gov/fulltext/EJ1083427.pdf.

2   Department for Education, *The Equality Act 2010 and Schools: Departmental Advice for School Leaders, School Staff, Governing Bodies and Local Authorities* (May 2014). Available at: https://assets.publishing.service.gov.uk/government/uploads/system/ uploads/attachment_data/file/315587/Equality_Act_Advice_Final.pdf.

discrimination that may be happening in your school. Not noticing your school's blind spots doesn't mean they don't exist. So, let's work together to notice what is happening and make sure every school is a genuinely safe and inclusive community.

To help, below are my five top tips for making your school LGBTQ+ friendly.

1. Use inclusive language

Even the most apparently insignificant words and phrases can be a powerful tool in the fight for – or against – inclusivity. Making small changes around inclusive language can, therefore, have a huge impact on making everyone feel not only accepted but welcome.

- Instead of greeting your staff team or students with, 'Good morning, ladies and gentlemen, boys and girls', say, 'Good morning, everyone'. With this, you have included all genders and identities without assuming everyone identifies with the gender they were assigned at birth.

- Challenge students and colleagues who continue to use phrases that diminish showing emotion or acting like a particular gender. For example: 'Man up', 'You throw like a girl' and 'Boys don't cry'.

- Stop organising students into boys' teams and girls' teams – find different ways.

- Avoid reinforcing gender stereotypes.

2. An LGBTQ+ friendly school is everyone's responsibility

It is a mistake to think that creating an LGBTQ+ friendly school should solely be the responsibility of the 'LGBTQ+ teacher' – it should be a collective responsibility. Head teachers, senior leadership teams (SLTs), teachers and the rest of the school community should be actively working together to promote an inclusive and diverse environment, ensuring all members of staff and students feel safe and can be their authentic selves.

- Continuing professional development and in-service training days could involve external speakers, offering your staff a refreshing voice and a different perspective.

- LGBTQ+ people experience the world differently to their heterosexual counterparts, and school leaders should give them a safe space to talk about their experiences, with the support of their LGBTQ+ allies.

3. Be proud of LGBTQ+ visibility

If you are showing a prospective same-sex family around your school, or an LGBTQ+ teacher comes for an interview, or a new student identifies as LGBTQ+ or does not know their sexuality, how will they know that your school is a safe and inclusive environment where they can be their authentic self?

- Give teachers a choice to wear LGBTQ+ badges/pins or have LGBTQ+ lanyards.

- Display the pride flag inside and outside your school.

- Show your visitors that you celebrate inclusion and diversity through well-maintained and curated displays celebrating LGBTQ+ stories and issues.

- Encourage LGBTQ+ teachers to make a network or support group where they can talk about LGBTQ+ issues and use this to show that LGBTQ+ voices matter.

- Have your SLT and staff go on a learning walk, where the focus is LGBTQ+ inclusion. Can you see it represented in your school?

4. Have an inclusive and diverse curriculum

Your curriculum should be well planned and deliberately tailored to minority groups and should not be left to chance. To avoid tokenism, these practices should be carefully planned and seen across all subject areas.

- Children's story books should include and promote different family dynamics, including same-sex couples, single parents, foster parents, disabled children and parents, families of colour, families of different religions and so on.

- Have word problems and challenges, in maths for example, that are inclusive of same-sex families. And instead of just 'Mrs Smith' or 'John', use names that come from a range of countries and heritages.

- In your presentations, ensure that the pictures you use show a range of minority groups.

- In your humanities curriculum, teach about colonisation and the impact of imperialism, and celebrate indigenous communities and customs.

- Diversify your set literary texts and other artistic achievements to offer a range of authors and artists, not just white, heterosexual men.

5. Educate yourself

I believe the best way to learn more about the LGBTQ+ community is to educate yourself. For this, as with all personal development and growth, you will need an open mind and the ability to be comfortable with being challenged. This commitment to professional development will help you overcome the fear – often in people who do not belong to a certain minority group – of making a mistake or unconsciously offending someone, or using a term or acronym that is outdated.

Read books and use organisations that specifically discuss LGBTQ+ voices in education and whole-school approaches, such as:

- Catherine Lee's *Courage in The Classroom: LGBT Teachers Share Their Stories* (2020).

- LGBTed co-founder Daniel Tomlinson-Gray's *Big Gay Adventures in Education* (2021).

- Elly Barnes and Anna Carlile's *How to Transform Your School into an LGBT+ Friendly Place* (2018).

- Jonathan Charlesworth's *That's So Gay! Challenging Homophobic Bullying* (2015).

- Shaun Dellenty's *Celebrating Difference: A Whole-School Approach to LGBT+ Inclusion* (2019).

- Andrew Moffat's book series for the No Outsiders programme.

- Pop'n'Olly, an LGBTQ+ equality educational resource for children, parents, carers and teachers.

- Centre for LGBTQ+ Inclusion in Education, part of Leeds Beckett University.

- *Pride & Progress*, a podcast that amplifies the voices of LGBTQ+ educators.

- The following organisations offer a plethora of teaching resources: Just Like Us, Educate & Celebrate, Schools Out, Stonewall Education, Mermaids UK, LGBTed, the LGBT Primary Hub and Diverse Educators.

Finally, when making cultural change in your school, it is important to avoid tokenism. If the only time you discuss LGBTQ+ rights or how to be anti-racist is for a week or a month as a bolt-on to your curriculum, this is superficial tokenism in action. Inclusion is part of who you are, not simply a tick on the curriculum. When all members of the community are on board – walking the walk, not just talking the talk – that is when real, positive and lasting change can happen.

Jared Cawley is a Year 6 class teacher and LGBTQ+ researcher, working within the international school sector.

Chapter 18
Moving Beyond the Label

Sara Alston

Often, both professionals' and parents' approach to a child with special needs starts with questions like 'What's wrong with them?' and 'Why can't they do that?' They want an explanation for the child's difficulties and believe that a diagnosis or label will reduce or maybe even cure them.

In reality, a diagnosis changes little. Knowing a child has a speech difficulty and struggles to articulate particular sounds makes no difference to their speech or ability to make themselves understood. What can make a difference is our response to their needs and the support they receive.

However, many teachers feel that they lack the necessary expertise. For them there is a hope that once a child is given a diagnosis, it will magically make the learning easier for them. For some teachers, it can even excuse inaction as they feel there is nothing that can be done, so they do not need to try to improve conditions for the child or promote their learning.

There is a belief among parents, and some professionals, that a diagnosis is not only the answer to a child's difficulties but also entitles them to extra support or even an education, health and care plan. Frustrated by the delays and staff shortages in child and adolescent mental health services, and special educational needs and disabilities (SEND) systems, parents who can afford to are increasingly bypassing the recognised channels and paying for a diagnosis, often without notifying or involving the school.[1]

---

1 Waiting lists of 18 months to 2 years are increasingly common in child and adolescent mental health services.

Further, the number of celebrities Instagramming their own learning difficulties and the ease of 'diagnosis' via 'Dr Google' means that, for some, a diagnostic label has almost become a status symbol.

Unfortunately, a diagnosis neither removes a child's challenges nor provides a ticket for extra support. There are many children on my SEND register who do not have or need a diagnosis. Equally, there are children throughout the school who have diagnoses of different kinds but are not on the SEND register because their needs can and should be met through quality-first teaching.

Schools cannot ignore children's needs because they do not have a diagnosis, nor should we provide children with additional support they don't need just because they do have one. The confusion about this adds to the pressures faced by many special educational needs coordinators (SENCOs) as parents search for support for their children in a system that is not easy to understand, even by those working within it.

These issues are complicated still further by some schools' responses to behaviour incidents. Clearly, no child should be penalised for behaviours that are part of a special need – medical or educational. Most school behaviour systems can accept that, for example, those with attention deficit hyperactivity disorder (ADHD) will, by the nature of their condition, fidget and fiddle more than their peers. But schools can struggle when dealing with incidents of aggression or sexualised behaviour. Even within so-called 'zero tolerance' settings, there needs to be a balance between the rigid enforcement of whole-school behaviour expectations and leniency allowable to those with special needs. In such cases, decision-makers too often fall back on a child's diagnosis and use this, rather than consideration of the child's needs, to moderate their disciplinary response. This means the child with a diagnosis may be supported, while a child without might face the full punitive force of the school's behaviour policy, even though they have identical needs.

Still worse are the occasions when the only way we can demonstrate a child has undiagnosed needs, and enable them to access support, is by allowing them to face some form of punitive response, such as a fixed-term exclusion.

Moreover, a diagnostic label does not tell us how to support a child in school, nor should it in the case of a medical diagnosis. The diagnosis can act as a signpost, but it does not provide the details of the support and adjustments a child needs to learn and be happy in school.

Indeed, in some circumstances, a diagnostic label can become a barrier to providing the appropriate support for a child by obscuring their individual needs. A diagnosis can be restrictive, leading to assumptions about a child's needs. Children are not robots to be fitted into neat diagnostic boxes. They produce a range of signs, symptoms and indicators which may reflect different educational needs or diagnoses, but will also be influenced by their personality, experiences and environment as well as their age, stage and gender. These will further change as the child develops and the educational demands placed on them vary. The support a child needs in primary school will be different to the support they need in secondary. For example, too often the needs of a child with a diagnosis of having an autism spectrum condition (ASC) are addressed based on a misconception that all children with that label have the same needs. But these diagnoses are on a continuum. The stereotypes and assumptions about need tend to focus on the extremes – the anti-social geniuses and *Rain Man*-type savants or locked-in non-verbal 'head bangers' – rather than recognising the full range of the triad of impairments associated with autism. The reality is that the majority of those with autism come somewhere between the extremes, but this nuance is often lost in the focus on the diagnostic label. This is not just true for those with ASC.

Confusingly, while many children given the same diagnosis present with different needs in the classroom, children with different diagnoses may present with similar needs. Difficulties with focus, sensory overload, word-finding and low self-esteem can all be characteristic for those with ASC, ADHD and dyslexia, or a combination of these difficulties. Schools need to be able to respond imaginatively to the child's individual needs and provide support focused on meeting them, not just respond to the diagnosis.

The risks involving diagnostic labels are clear to many SENCOs. But faced with pressure from senior leaders, other staff and parents, too often we allow the label to overwhelm our knowledge of the individual. This means that much-needed support and resources end up directed to meet the description of the difficulty, rather than the child's actual challenges and needs.

In my view, there are only three significant reasons for a school to support seeking a diagnosis for a child:

- To access funding.

- To give us direction in understanding and helping a child and their needs – because this is not known, despite our efforts.

- Most importantly, to support a child's self-esteem by providing an explanation of their difficulties which they themselves can understand, or to support the parents to understand that there are issues with their child despite their best parenting efforts.

I am not against diagnoses of special educational needs and have personally benefitted from a diagnosis of dyslexia. As a child, my diagnosis enabled my parents, teachers and me to understand that there was a reason for my significant difficulties with reading and writing, and that it was not just that I was lazy and/or stupid. But that alone was not enough to make the difference to my educational future. It required a focused response that considered my particular needs, not all of which fit the standardised descriptors of dyslexia.

SENCOs need confidence and support from other school leaders to move beyond the label and see the whole child. This can be difficult when facing demands from anxious parents and over-stressed teachers. We need whole-school approaches that both emphasise children's strengths as well as working to diminish their barriers to learning. An overemphasis on 'labels' can inhibit this, obscure the child's needs from view and prevent them and their teachers from gaining the support they really need.

Sara Alston is a practising SENCO and an independent SEND and safeguarding consultant and trainer with over 30 years' teaching experience. She writes regular articles and blogs about SEND and safeguarding issues. She is the co-author of The Inclusive Classroom: A New Approach to Differentiation (Bloomsbury, 2021) and author of Working Effectively with Your TA (Bloomsbury, forthcoming 2023).

Chapter 19

'Always Stay Below the Radar, Mr B, Always Stay Below the Radar'

David Boehme

You do not really know each other as you are new to the school and you are a teaching assistant (TA) from an agency. You are here to support children with special educational needs and disabilities (SEND), rather than a permanent teacher like your colleague. (You probably have to go in a year or in two.) You are chatting, as colleagues do, but something is playing on your mind – do you mention that you have just been diagnosed with Asperger's syndrome?

This was the position I found myself in not that long ago at a school in Germany (but it could have been any school, anywhere), and I was struggling to work out what to do for the best. My initial plan was easy. First, I tell the agency. Later, I share it with parents and then, finally, with the school management. After that, if necessary, I would share my secret with my colleagues but only those who I felt I knew well enough to trust, which, at that moment, was not many. I was not sleeping too well at that time, as you can perhaps imagine.

I arranged a conversation with the *Geschäftsführer* (senior mangement, or boss) during which I would summarise the key points of my diagnosis, list my workplace needs and clearly identify the strengths that my disability brings as an assistant for young people on SEND support. But for various complicated reasons, that face-to-face conversation did not take place.

Ruling out talking to the school management, I then considered whether to share my diagnosis with the parents. But what if that upset some of them or even their children? The sleepless nights continued. I wanted to be honest, really I did, but I just couldn't second-guess the consequences of my 'coming out'.

Then something interesting happened. An autistic student said to me, quite by chance, 'You know, my strategy is to stand out as little as possible. Always stay below the radar, Mr B., always stay below the radar.' It was a short statement by a young boy, a clear declaration of how he had got through his young life as an autistic person so far. For me, it was a major epiphany. I enjoyed my first good night's sleep for weeks once I made up my mind to follow this student's example – I stayed below the radar.

Although this newly gained position helped my levels of anxiety, I still had a nagging feeling that I was missing something. What if 'below the radar' almost meant 'below my potential'? What if I was missing an opportunity to actually help people like me, in the classroom and in the staffroom? By choosing to remain 'normal', I had chosen *not* to be the one ideally positioned to offer training for other TAs and teachers on autism at school. What's more, I had chosen not to be the one to change the school's wider perceptions of what autism entailed – perceptions demonstrated in the two examples I will now describe.

A teacher was told that she was going to have one more student with Asperger's syndrome in her class, making a grand total of two 'inclusion children'. Her reaction, while rolling her eyes: 'Great! Then I have two of *them* sitting in here with me.' I was not shocked. When support and the necessary resources for adequate training are not forthcoming, mainstream teachers can struggle to support children with specific needs within a class of 30 children. Read that line again though: 'Then I have two of *them* sitting in here with me.' How do you react? How would you feel if you were one of 'them'? Although I understood this statement, it felt strange, or rather I felt affected by it, deeply. From then on, I never thought of telling anyone at school about my diagnosis. Or my needs. Or my strengths. It was another example that persuaded me once and for all to follow the boy's advice and keep well and truly below the radar.

On another occasion I was supporting a PE lesson and the teacher said to me: 'Go for a walk with this student and take that student with you too. I need to get on with the lesson.' This time I was shocked. Unlike the teacher who was going to be stretched by the extra tasks involved in having that one extra student (inclusion/integration/differentiated teaching, etc.), the PE teacher had many possibilities when it came to integrating those children into the lesson. Yes, it would require some extra preparation, but – more important than that – there surely has to be an interest, a professionally curious commitment to understand what an autistic student is capable of and what preferences they may have. In this incident, the desire to learn about autism was non-existent, as was any interest in the students and their needs.

So, I remained under the radar at that school and remain there still. My deepest wish is to find myself in a school that welcomes autistic staff, where there is no gossip about colleagues with disabilities in the staffroom. Who would not love a school that celebrates the vital role autistic people like me can play in assisting that school's autistic students, coaching them, role modelling for them by sharing their own experiences as actually autistic?

So here is a big wish from this tiny voice – see the able, not the label. Be curious. Learn. Commit to teach *all* the students in your class. And when you complain about how difficult your students are, or how challenging it is to have several of 'them' in the classroom, remember that one of 'them' might be sitting next to you in the staffroom, quietly, under the radar.

David Boehme is an educator and has been working with autistic children and young people since his further training as an inclusion specialist. He is also part of a tiny but talented team at a counselling centre. In the midst of the COVID-19 pandemic, he started to mentor autistic adults and is now initiating empowerment groups.

Chapter 20

Tiny Steps for Better Well-Being

Nerys Hughes

Cumulatively small decisions, choices, actions, make a very big difference.

Jane Goodall[1]

Mental health is a big challenge with some big – and scary – statistics. For example, one in six school-aged children experience mental health problems.[2] This means that mental health services and support systems are often overstretched. According to the Centre for Mental Health, it takes 10 years for a child to receive specific help from when they first display symptoms.[3]

The emotional health of teachers is under pressure too with 76% of education professionals having experienced behavioural, psychological or physi-

---

1   Marianne Schnall, Exclusive interview with Dr Jane Goodall, *HuffPost* (1 June 2010). Available at: https://www.huffpost.com/entry/exclusive-interview-with_b_479894.

2   University of Exeter, One in six children has probable mental disorder in 2021 – continuing 2020 peak (30 September 2021). Available at: https://www.exeter.ac.uk/news/research/title_879721_en.html.

3   Centre for Mental Health, Fact sheet: children and young people's mental health (27 April 2022). Available at: https://www.centreformentalhealth.org.uk/fact-sheet-children-and-young-peoples-mental-health.

cal symptoms due to work pressures, compared to 60% of UK employees in other sectors.[4] What's more, 47% have experienced depression, anxiety or panic attacks due to work and these statistics are only getting worse. Reported experience of insomnia has increased from 41% to 56%, irritability or mood swings from 37% to 51%, tearfulness from 31% to 44%, forgetfulness from 27% to 41% and difficulty concentrating from 27% to 40%. Shockingly, all these increases are noted in the short period between 2017 and 2018, so this is before you factor in the personal and professional stress of the COVID-19 pandemic.

This tiny voice is saying we have a big problem. We need change.

The good news is that mental health is recoverable and, like all the big challenges we face, it is the little things we do that can make the biggest of impacts; there are so many changes we can make to support our wellbeing. Moreover, the solutions that work for us are also beneficial across a whole school community, supporting learning and improving outcomes for everyone. So, take a little time to digest the numbers and the statistics, but know that we have got this; we can grow and with realistic changes and small steps, you can make a very big difference.

Before I share some suggestions, a quick word about boundaries and the importance of saying no. I was in a Team Around a Child meeting recently where a mental health professional suggested to a special educational needs coordinator (SENCO) that she should buy a book on cognitive behavioural therapy to help a young person who was continuing to self-harm and make attempts on their life. I asked the SENCO if they were comfortable providing cognitive behavioural strategies with this child and if they felt they had the skills to support this student in this direct specialist method of intervention. Her response was both correct and brave – 'No!' The SENCO did not have this particular skill set – and nor should she be expected to, as it is highly specialised. Nor was it her role anyway. This SENCO was managing her own job very, very well, and the child needed specific and specialised intervention from qualified mental health professionals, not from her and a book. Her honest answer to the all-important question 'Are you comfortable with this?' was at least a step in the right direction.

---

4   Education Support Partnership, *Teacher Wellbeing Index 2018* (2018). Available at: http://downloads2.dodsmonitoring.com/downloads/Misc_Files/teacher_wellbeing_index_2018.pdf.

Ask yourself the same question as I share the following strategies with you – 'Do I feel comfortable and secure in my ability to do this?' – and remember that our own capacity will fluctuate and change, so give yourself room and space to do what fits with you. Authenticity is essential to human connection, so find the tools that make you feel comfortable, the ones that feel exciting and rewarding, the ones that sing to you.

Tiny suggestion 1: It is essential to achieve self-regulation before attempting to enable co-regulation for your students

'What is co-regulation?' you may ask. Well, it's the first tool in your mental health toolkit. We all need some form of co-regulation and it is the very essence of social connection.[5] In short, we model how to manage challenges by demonstrating how we manage our own challenges. We enable calm through modelling calm. We enable resolution by modelling resolution. We demonstrate self-regulation by being honest in our own feelings. By being in control of our own emotional reactions, we can support the children who need help in managing their emotions. This is co-regulation – the interactions that provide regulatory support within our relationships. This may include empathy, providing a stable and safe environment, structured routines and logical consequences, modelling self-regulation skills and providing scaffolding as we teach our students these vital skills.

Tiny steps for your classroom

Take time to discuss the emotional meaning of our own and our students' experiences. An example may be: 'I am concerned that we have not managed to finish the text as quickly as I had hoped today, so I am thinking we may save questions for the end of today's session and not do them as we go. Let's give that a try.' Model asking at the end how they felt it went and

---

5   You might have experienced an aspect of co-regulation known as 'emotional contagion' – those times when you have laughed for no reason just because someone else is laughing.

if this strategy would work at other times, demonstrating that the ability to adapt and reflect is a strong personal skill, especially when things don't go as planned.

We can also model experiences. An example may be: 'Can you all please help me? My head is really hurting because it has been such a busy, noisy day. Could we take 5 minutes with the lights turned off and just do a little breathing exercise together before we go back to the task? I think this will really help us work better.' We are demonstrating that we all occasionally need to 'take five', that a moment of quiet and calm is valuable to us all and that even grown-ups can feel overwhelmed. Asking honestly and calmly for time out is a far greater tool than losing your temper or just wishing for the day (or your career) to end.

Tiny suggestion 2:
Remember that movement improves attention, concentration and mood

The use of aerobic activity has been shown to improve academic achievement, especially in children,[6] and enhance cognitive abilities such as learning, memory and attentional and executive processes.[7] It takes around 15 minutes of aerobic activity to increase blood flow and make sufficient cardiac impact; however, even 5–10 minutes of activity across a day will impact mood and attention for learning.[8]

Note, too, that the benefits of aerobic movement are so well recognised as health-enabling factors that the US Department of Health and Human Services and the Department of Health and Social Care in the UK

---

6   Laura Mandolesi, Arianna Polverino, Simone Montuori et al., Effects of physical exercise on cognitive functioning and wellbeing: biological and psychological benefits, *Frontiers in Psychology* 9 (2018): 509. DOI. 10.3389/fpsyg.2018.00509.

7   Centre for Mental Health, Fact sheet.

8   Aylin Mehren, Jale Özyurt, Alexandra P. Lam et al., Acute effects of aerobic exercise on executive function and attention in adult patients with ADHD, *Frontiers in Psychiatry* 10 (2019): 132. DOI. 10.3389/fpsyt.2019.00132/full.

have committed budget and time to promoting these tools as part of their health-promotion and illness-prevention strategies.[9]

It can be really interesting to take a little time to observe your children in free play. How many actively engage in motor-based activity? By nature, younger children are driven to participate in cycles of heightened activity and rest. Like little jumping beans, they are likely to engage in more sensory motor-based play like climbing, running and tag. Little ones who do not participate in sensory motor play are at more risk of missing motor milestones or developing maladaptive motor patterns. These children are more likely to experience disrupted self-regulation and have less attuned interoception – the connection between our brains and bodies which tells us when we are tired, hungry, thirsty, hot, cold and needing the toilet. Sensory motor play encourages and strengthens the connections that help us know and respond to what we need.

When we reflect on older students, the amount of time that they engage in physical activity can be reduced or increased depending on their habits and interests. Children who do not participate in physical activity may be more prone to anxiety and depression.[10] Knowing your students' preferences and abilities will help you pitch the activity just right so as not to embarrass or set a student up to fail. Making sure that movement for regulation is not competitive helps because it means a child can be more present in their own body experience, not focused on trying to be better than someone else. Encouraging the students to think about what their body is asking of them today is a great start too.

---

9   US Department of Health and Human Services, *Physical Activity Guidelines for Americans*, 2nd edn, p. 39. Available at: https://health.gov/sites/default/files/2019-09/Physical_Activity_Guidelines_2nd_edition.pdf; Department of Health and Social Care, *UK Chief Medical Officers' Physical Activity Guidelines* (2019). Available at: https://assets.publishing.service.gov.uk/government/uploads/system/uploads/attachment_data/file/832868/uk-chief-medical-officers-physical-activity-guidelines.pdf.

10   Dr Zhu was the first author on a 2019 study of 35,000 children and adolescents aged from 6 to 17 in the United States, which found that those who reported doing no exercise were twice as likely to have mental health problems, particularly related to anxiety and depression, compared with those who met the exercise guidelines; see Perri Klass, The benefits of exercise for children's mental health, *New York Times* (2 March 2020). Available at: https://www.nytimes.com/2020/03/02/well/family/the-benefits-of-exercise-for-childrens-mental-health.html.

Introducing movement-based activity into the school day can also be a way of supporting transitions, providing punctuation for the beginnings and endings. This can be a problematic time for some students. The benefits to learning far outweigh any so-called 'lost' learning time. Of course, new routines take a while to become established – about a term, I have found – but do persevere and the small wins will start to mount up. Below are some ideas to get you started.

Tiny steps for your classroom

When kids are fidgeting, scrunching their bodies, slouching over the desk, I would say they are telling you it's time to throw in a little stretch-and-wake routine or some chair-based actions. These are all good ways of getting kids 'back in their bodies' and 'back in their brains', ready for learning. Movement for mood and attention should be integrated every day and throughout each day and is just as important in secondary schools as it is in primaries.

Flash cards are a great device to encourage the sort of movement needed and there are some wonderful resources available that are affordable, or even free. We have a system called 'Lollipops', in which there is a picture of an action on one side of a card and written instructions on the other, which are read out to the class. We simply stick the cards to lollipop sticks, pop them in a cup on the desks and then pull them out – or let the children choose them – as needed.

Other forms of proprioceptive engagement include stamping our feet, stretching our arms over our heads or even the simple act of hugging ourselves.[11] Setting up task-based activities that involve lifting, pulling, carrying and sweeping, for example, can be ways to have children moving while also giving them jobs and roles that help them feel a sense of belonging (as well as getting your classroom tidied!).

---

11   Proprioception is the nervous system's response to movement input from the activation of muscles, tendons and joints. This system helps us know where our body is in space, for example. Input received by our brain through the proprioceptive system can be organising and calming.

We also have the vestibular system to think about too.[12] Linear input such as rocking and rowing can have a calming effect, whereas rotary activities (e.g. roundabouts, spinners and dancing) serve to excite and stimulate.

Once you know what impact you want and what sort of activity will achieve it, you are well equipped for keeping children alert, balanced and focused throughout the school day.

Tiny suggestion 3: Tap into the proven power of mindfulness

The first key to mindfulness is breathing, and it can be really useful to observe the breathing quality and patterns going on in your class. Many of us hold our breath when we are challenged mentally or physically, without even realising that we are doing it. For children with motor difficulties, we see this when they are trying to stabilise, write or sit still. Children who are prone to anxiety often use erratic and shallow breathing cycles. You may see a child taking a breath mid-word or not being able to breathe fluently over the course of a sentence. We need oxygen to think, to move, to sit comfortably and, most importantly, to feel calm. Just hold your breath for a few seconds and see how disorientating it can be.

Tiny steps for your classroom

The '3-4-5 Breathing Technique' is a really simple, but effective, little calming strategy. Simply breathe in for a count of 3, hold your breath for a count of 4 then breath out for a count of 5. Do this between three and ten times, then reflect on the change you observe in how you are sitting, how you feel and your attention and concentration. You will be amazed!

Taking time to breathe with your students throughout the day will boost their attention and well-being. It is also a powerful tool to help with the

---

12   The vestibular system is located in the inner ear, signalling to the brain the speed and direction we are moving in. It plays a role in balance and posture, and is responsible for motion sickness.

co-regulation between you and your class. Take it up a level with singing or other rhythmic activity like clapping out sounds together. Spending time in a rhythmic activity as a group develops bonding and connection is the bedrock to good mental health. It will also enable you to be a calmer and more grounded teacher too.

Breathing helps us become calm, but we still need something to address the worries in our head now that we are in a better state to think about them effectively. We can do this in so many different ways. One tool we often use in classrooms is a 'Thoughts and Worries Box'. Children anonymously write down what is on their minds and put it in the box. We then dedicate time daily or weekly to review these concerns, working as a class to find strategies to help. It is always worth working with the children to put in place a contract or agreement here in order to feel safe sharing our worries as a group too. Check the thoughts before you share them with the class and make sure you guide the students to sensible and kind solutions. Establishing the contract with clear expectations usually goes a long way towards ensuring students feel comfortable with the activity.

Other calming strategies include zen doodling, mindful colouring and tools for visualisation such as drawing a safe space, making a mood board or taking the class through a guided visualisation.

An important point to make here is that we do need to reflect on students who may have experienced, or be experiencing, trauma. Always support students in opting in and opting out of any mindfulness activity. Remember, we are asking children to be present in their body at that moment so teaching them that they can say no and that they have body autonomy are empowering lessons to learn.

Tiny suggestion 4:
Look after yourself and be present too

Teaching can be extremely stressful and thinking about how we can improve our own flow, mindfulness and movement opportunities can only enhance our day. Take time out for yourself and find some small steps that work for you. Before you attempt to reach out and fill the emotional cups of others, take the steps you need to take to fill your own.

Moving, breathing and noticing yourself all help, as does finding one thing that you like and ensuring you experience it every day. Play for grown-ups is so vital too; a game of cards, staff dodgeball or five-a-side football, team lunches – anything that helps you find the time to have fun, to laugh, to breathe and to connect is really powerful. Invest some time in noting down five things that you find rewarding, that support your well-being and self-esteem. These could be anything from walking, laughing and art to abseiling, seeing friends or volunteering in your community. Find what supports your well-being and then perhaps share that with your students and ask them to write their own list.

Through starting small, we can all work together to bring about joy, belonging and a sense of achievement and pride in what we do and who we are. After all, little changes can make a big difference, just as tiny voices can make a big noise.

Nerys Hughes is the founder and clinical director of Whole Child Therapy, London (WCT). WCT is one of the first interdisciplinary social enterprise clinics in the UK, providing occupational therapy, speech therapy, osteopathy, nutritional therapy, play therapy and family support for families, schools and charities.

Chapter 21
All Kids Included

Liv Dara

All my life I've been sick and tired.

Now I'm sick and tired of being sick and tired.

Fannie Lou Hamer[1]

You take to your bed, a few days after the world noticed George Floyd was gone. The case rakes up remnants of the feelings you had when Trayvon Martin's name kept appearing in your feeds[2] – 'This is too much' and 'Nothing will change'.

In recent times, you have heard so many names. Deborah Danner. Michelle Cuseaux. Atatiana Jefferson. Botham Jean. Rasharn Charles. You long ago ceased watching the videos that so often crossed your timeline. There had been too many of them. The final moments of 12-year-old Tamir Rice, and then Walter Scott, would be the last times you were able to stomach these numerous 'one-off' incidents. And now George Floyd.

You ignore that hashtag.

For days.

There is nothing to suggest that this time will be any different.

---

1 Maegan P. Brooks and Davis W. Houck (eds.), *The Speeches of Fannie Lou Hamer: To Tell It Like It Is* (Jackson, MS: University Press of Mississippi, 2011).

2 See https://www.ebony.com/tag/trayvon-martin/.

But the news keeps coming and it is too much.

You switch the devices off.

Three days later when you log back on, something has shifted.

People – lots of people – are still talking. This time, the hashtag had not been relegated to Black Twitter.

In April 2020, we learn that Black women and men are up to four times more likely to die of COVID-19 than White people. Anti-Blackness and COVID-19. Two pandemics at once.

Silence.

No extra measures put in place. No structural change on the horizon.

The people flocked to the beaches; you could not fathom.

You survive the virus in March, but you are not well and you will not feel well for months and months. You still need to catch public transport. Some people seem proud of their disregard for the safety of themselves and others. You watch this all unfold.

You see the ambulances outside neighbours' homes. Weekly.

There are further hashtags.

Continually.

One week we have #BlackOutTuesday. Black squares replace profile pictures. Not quite everywhere though.

A White friend contacts you out of the blue. You never hear from them again.

Most say nothing at all.

Silence is golden.

A Time (Not So) Long Ago

You are reminded of that night in the fish and chip shop, where you were sent on an errand with your eldest foster brother.

One moment you are happy! The next you are frozen.

He was beaten up by the two White boys who had been playing an arcade game.

You cannot recall any sound, just the awareness that the man is preparing an order, with his head down.

While a Black boy is being beaten up by two White boys.

You live in a house with two White boys.

Head down, food served. And then … nothing. You are 5.

You are not present in the moments your foster mother's son takes his own life. Was it Christmas Eve or Christmas Day? You remember your own mother wailing downstairs. Upstairs alone, colouring a red vehicle and then, silence.

There are groups of older kids who are into fashion. They are a presence. They wear brightly coloured clothes and hairstyles. You would later learn they had special names: punks, skinheads.

Of course, there are good times. After-school clubs where you practise on the pogo stick (you could never stay upright for more than a few seconds). Or cross-stitching indoors. There is Sunday school and berry-picking for homemade jam and the time of your lives at the caravan park. There is nothing unusual about your family except the pain and tears.

Your teacher is Princess Diana, or so you think. She rides a moped. You get to see the cavalcade of the real princess. You are too small to see anything more than her blonde hair. Afterwards, you can't believe how excited you'd been to be left with nothing but memories of hair. But still, royalty.

Leaving the foster home, you vow never to return.

You attend a new school. Here, too, all the kids are White but they are bilingual. They speak English and variations on a theme. 'Suck your mom'.

There is poverty, but there is joy, oh! You play football and attend cookery club and your favourite teacher bakes flapjacks on Fridays, for the win.

You have two friends by the name of K. One, your best friend, is blonde and has huge dimples when she smiles and you spend so much time at her house. Her little sisters are cute and her step-dad is rock-star cool. One day he takes you both to Woolworths and manages to swipe you a Creme Egg each. You will remember this each time you are followed by security guards.

The other K is everyone's on-again, off-again friend. She is slightly dirty and often threatens to batter people. Everybody threatens that, so no one takes any notice of her. K has an older brother who sometimes picks her up from school. He is brown-skinned. One afternoon she invites you home and you think, 'why not'? When you enter the front door, her mother exclaims 'Urgh! Blackie!' You are 10.

Incidents gather momentum.

Your English teacher, the one you really like, the one who introduced you to Anne Frank, says you have graffitied all over a desk. You have not. He does not listen. This goes on for a Very Long Time. Then, in front of the whole class, he tells you something you will never forget: 'You couldn't have done it, because you weren't sitting there last week.' He then proceeds to blame you anyway, shooting down anyone who speaks up for you.

What can you say? You are 12.

You are, for the most part, the only Black child in class. You could hang around with the boring-but-smart kids or the cool-but-mean ones. You choose the latter. Cue 3 years of put-downs, jibes about untrendy clothes and racist comments about their own Black boyfriends. Home is not home and you do not want to be alone 24/7. You do not yet know any teachers you feel safe enough to confide in. After school, you dance. Dance and dance and dance. And draw. There are no books or toys so your only other entertainment/company is the TV. You see a lot of stereotypical characters.

In Year 9, the Black boy from the class next door is moved to yours. Because of behaviour. He is a bit naughty, a bit annoying. But so are all the boys. There is the time the French teacher tells him he is moving around like 'a monkey in a cage'. The following week she does it again. Your White friends giggle next to you.

Then there are all the times the PE teacher harms so many of you, but particularly the Black boy and you.

(One day, the Black boy loans you his *Straight Outta Compton* vinyl. He is excited to be sharing this with you and you feel chuffed. You remember his smile – like he was introducing you to *real* Black culture. On the way home you take great care not to damage the record. You're a bit giddy with excitement because, oh my God, *swear words*! The first time you heard a Black person using the N-word, it felt like you had been stabbed in the chest. You are a liner-note-reading geek. And even after all the murder and misogyny, they thanked the Almighty. You are confused.)

There is the silence of all the teachers who must have known – but said nothing.

In Year 10, the Black boy leaves the school completely. He claims he is picked on by staff.

One day, your two best friends at the time – one White, one Black and of mixed heritage – take to calling you the N-word. Publicly. Repeatedly. Home life is poor. You alternate between these kids' homes each night. Where else can you go? What can you say?

Silence. You are 14.

You discover *Word Up!*, *The Voice* and *The Source*, among other things. You will learn new names and old traumas. Emmett Till. The Tuskegee Experiment. Ricky Reel. Rolan Adams. Stephen Lawrence. Amadou Diallo. Sean Bell.

You stay at school, into sixth form, because you aren't ready to move on and some kind teachers have given you the confidence to think you might one day become something. Maybe a science teacher. You want to help the poor kids like you who no one believed in.

You hear people say things they never would in front of the kids from the hostels.

You are used to being cussed out, so do not really notice that you are constantly referred to as 'useless'.

The hostel is where you learn to act tough and where you learn to rage.

You need to see and hear things that make you feel better about yourself and your life. You read things that say different groups of people are not naturally meant to be around one another. They will never get along. Dating outside your race? Wrong. Dating your own gender? Wrong. Dating your own gender from outside your race? The Worst.

This period doesn't last, thankfully, but it gives you an insight into the far-right mind. You learn some compassion for them, particularly when you learn that a number of these young people, like Dylann Roof, are probably on the autistic spectrum, and as such are vulnerable to manipulation by terror organisations.

You learn all the ways your people have been harmed. You learn that very few people are trustworthy. Around this time, when you are having to buy bus passes and food, you notice the ways you are blatantly followed in corner shops, chemists and supermarkets. You notice all the times you are stared at. The way women grab their bags at the mere presence of you. Your favourite teacher does this to you once. And one day, so will one of your bosses.

In the hostels are mainly Black kids. There are Asian girls and a couple of White kids. Each of the four hostels you live in has a similar make-up. You never see this reality reflected in Christmas homelessness appeals.

You are mocked for staying in your room all the time, but how else would you be safe? You hang out with White M who has all Black friends and seems really, really cool. Then M calls her boyfriend a 'monkey'.

You meet a few White girls who date Black boys and call them 'monkeys', 'Black bastards' and worse, to your face. They cry real tears when their boyfriends leave them. The White kids call their Asian friends the P-word behind their backs. One day, in the common room, a White boy says the

P-word and you say nothing. Someone realises L is in the room. She laughs it off. You freeze in your seat. What kind of friend are you?

There is fun though. You dance and you draw. You rap with A and share food with L, who is one of your best friends. It is the time of Cross Colours and contact lenses. A parent of one of the Asian girls has discovered where she is and has camped opposite the building for 2 weeks. You take turns buying her stuff from the shops, where you are followed. The Asian girl from Scotland sits way too close and … Bye!

W arrives with green eyes. You are not sure if he is very dark for a mixed boy, or very light for a Black boy. You think he may just be a bounty. (You are rather judgemental for a homeless person.) He is in fact none of these things; simply fashion-conscious and experimental.

C will give up the goods loudly to randoms. As will lots of girls. They will be called names. You worry they will be hurt.

S plays music until 4 a.m. You fall asleep in lessons. No one asks why you're tired.

Everyone loves G, who is dark with blonde-tinged locks and from Liverpool. None of you have met a Black Liverpudlian before. He is like a little no-home-having celebrity. You have to remind yourself to stop staring at him while he minds his Black Liverpudlian business.

D is quietly wonderful. He is the one that introduces you to dub poetry and Radio 4. 'Bun Mi Spliff' blows your mind, though the presence of sweet, gentle W will put you off drugs for life, given his penchant for uncontrollable rage whenever he can't get access to any. Years later you will learn about the very real connection between marijuana use and psychosis in some people.

J takes to meditating in the common room with the TV on. Everybody laughs and she doesn't seem to notice. At precisely 2 a.m., she terrifies everyone in the three-storey building with her screaming. The two mean girls had offered to trim her hair shoulder length and instead given her a crew cut. A member of staff who knew her from before is concerned. Something had happened to her. Later on, she has what they call a 'breakdown'. You don't really know what that is, but you all stop laughing.

E is sweet until she offers to stab you in your eye. But you know it's not her, it's the aerosol talking. In a few years, a girl with the same name will be stabbed to death in a women's facility out in the sticks.

All you kids can get along.

If only you had somewhere to go/glow.

If you weren't so invisible to the world.

You will get your A levels and moooove.

You will go to university and suffer multiple health issues. You will stop drawing and find there is no room for dance. No one explains to you that halls are not like hostels. You cannot sleep in that room all year round. No one can help you because 'We have never had a student in your position before.' This, you feel, is a somewhat inadequate response.

You will leave after the first year, after exhausting all of your alternative accommodation options.

You will start over. On sign-up day at your new college, a careers advisor – a complete stranger – will inform you that journalism is unrealistic for you. You wonder how she knows this.

You get your A levels and, working three jobs, moving multiple times in search of stability, scrape your way through your degree.

You accidentally land a job in special educational needs and disabilities (SEND) and are called a 'Black c***' by a 7-year-old. The (White) teacher and (White) teaching assistant say nothing. Awkward.

You will get used to being talked down to, stared at and blamed for things you did not do. You will get used to people thinking you lack intelligence. People being angry at your joy. You reduce yourself. You are expert at saying nothing. You learn to seethe silently. Sometimes you will explode. No one will guess or know why.

Years and years of abuse, gaslighting and dismissal of your lived experiences will lead you to self-harm, to A&E. You have lost multiple members of your family to mental illness. You know how to fight. You have had to, from the first breath. But why is it so hard to get others to see? Or care? Maybe it's impossible. So, you move on. There are good people in the world. In education. Those willing to be challenged and make themselves vulnerable to the distress of others, including those they would normally cross the street to avoid.

We know what's up. Our stories, our lives, our children are worth fighting for. And if we are true educators, all children are our children.

Your years in hostels and your years at ChildLine have taught you to look deeper than the surface when it comes to helping young people. They get it. They are already making the changes you dreamed of seeing years ago. And you are glad you are still here, to witness the spectacle.

Over your time in education, and elsewhere, you witness many conversations. It's just that the subject of the conversation is rarely in the room.

Muslim-boy conversations.

Queer-people conversations.

Aggressive-parent conversations.

Mental health patients will call you every racist word under the sun. Staff members will often do nothing. They often make comments and jokes themselves. They will use the N-word over and over and over.

Words are just words.

When you try to explain, on an individual basis, what it feels like to be the subject of racist incidents, non-Black people will try and correct you. They see each individual incident as a stand-alone. They don't see the accumulation of years – decades – of harm. You try to be as polite as possible, yet some will still take more offence at the calling out of harm than at the harm itself.

You will learn, as an adult, that you have been living your whole life with an undiagnosed learning disability. You are neurodivergent.

This explains a lot!

This will not fix things.

You learn that the experiences of disabled people of colour are also hidden. More so. You are a private person. But if you do not speak up, who will? Who will advocate for the younger ones?

And So Here We Are.

Before the summer of 2020, there were hashtags, there were names, there was sometimes video footage. Ricky Reel. Rolan Adams. Amadou Diallo. Tamir Rice. Aiyana Stanley-Jones. Stephen Lawrence.

The current focus upon adverse childhood experiences and trauma-informed approaches is a start. But we have not gone all the way. Any approach that does not fully explore the systemic nature of racism and hatred will not achieve its stated goals. There are multiple forms of discrimination that children and young people face in today's Britain. Abuse ('jokes') directed at Roma/Traveller communities, Islamophobia, anti-Semitism, LGBTQIA+ prejudice or the disdain for working-class communities, some of whom are of colour. There is so much to do.

Of course, you fail. Repeatedly. But you have the courage to care.

You are learning to speak up, perhaps truly, for the first time.

The children trust in you and you admire them.

Things are changing.

Most do not care. Some are actively annoyed. Others are afraid.

For those who believe that racism can and should be kept out of the class-room, consider America. There, the rates of suicide for Black children and young people have risen 73% since 1991.[3] The rates of Black children dying by suicide are double those of White children.

We can do better.

---

3   Jeffrey A. Bridge, Lisa M. Horowitz, Cynthia A. Fontanella et al., Age-related racial disparity in suicide rates among US youths from 2001 through 2015, *JAMA Pediatrics* 172(7) (2018): 697.

We must.

All children deserve a childhood free from the traumas of systemic violence, however that manifests its ugly self – generational poverty, below-standard housing, food insecurity, actual bodily harm.

The concept of inclusive education and SEND provision within mainstream schools owes a large debt to those unsung Black parents and educators who fought to have their children removed from those so-called 'Schools for the Educationally Subnormal', just as the African-American civil rights movement paved the way for disability rights and entry of non-Black migrants from around the world into the States.

There is a new awareness that unity, not separation, is what benefits the individual. There is no reason to believe, as some have argued, that protecting the rights of marginalised groups means denying the rights of others. There are enough to go around.

COVID-19 has reminded us of our interdependence. I remain hopeful.

The world has rallied for racial justice. Young people from Flint, Michigan, to Manchester and Montreal are speaking out.

There is no time for despair, because love wins in the end.

No, really.

Love *Wins* In The End.

All kids included.

Liv Dara has worked in education, mental health and third sector fields, including as a volunteer for ChildLine. She wants to see a fairer world for children of colour, children in care, and all marginalised and vulnerable children and young people.

Part IV

Tiny Voices Talk About Professional and Personal Development

What values matter most to you? What are your hopes and where do you dream of being in 5 years, 10 years? By the time you reach retirement?

I don't know about you, but over my many years of teaching I have stood up in front of countless children and asked them to consider their values, their desires, their hopes and dreams – but how often do we ask those things of ourselves? Yet, in my opinion, all are intrinsically linked to our professional development.

As I mentioned earlier, I think it is vital for teachers to engage with professional development throughout their careers – education is ever evolving and we need to evolve with it. But I also think that we need to prioritise our personal development as it is this that will dictate the direction we need to go in – and that's not always up!

All too often in education, we talk about the career ladder and often feel that our value is attached to the rung that we are on. The higher the rung, the better we feel (theoretically). How would it be if we flung the ladder away and instead created our own climbing wall? This was an idea that my friend Nic shared with me and it profoundly changed the way I perceived success, development and the direction I chose to go in within education.

The foundation stones of my wall are my values – those things that really matter to me – and the more deeply set they are, the stronger my wall is. The wall itself has many different paths and I can go up, down, sideways, diagonally – in fact, I can go any way that suits me. I should mention, however, that the paths created themselves once I knew who I was, where I wanted to go and what I wanted to do. I think it is so important that we know who we are as educators, as leaders and as colleagues, as this determines the directions we will travel in. That's why I wanted to include Matt's chapter 'Who Am I?' (Chapter 22). Who you are determines so much and yet, as Matt points out, very often he is met with silence when he asks this question of his clients.

The other two chapters in this section are on coaching and mentoring – both of which hold such important places in the educational world. It is so important that our student and early career teachers are mentored and guided by teachers who have trodden that path. It is equally important that as educators we are coached so that we can find our own answers and feel empowered in the roles we take on.

Chapter 22

Who Am I?

Matt Dechaine

Authenticity is a collection of choices that we have to make every day. It's about the choice to show up and be real. The choice to be honest. The choice to let our true selves be seen.

Brené Brown[1]

When embarking on a coaching relationship with a teacher or a head teacher, I always ask two big questions: 'Who are you as a human being?' and 'Who are you as an educator?' More often than not, I am met with silence. It is rare for anyone to answer these questions immediately but, while there is nothing wrong with taking some time to reflect on them, our immediate responses can help identify our essence, our core values, who we really are. They help us answer that most important of questions – who am I?

I've thought a lot about such questions and continue to do so. They are questions none of us address often enough or for long enough. Spending our time in the busyness and business of life, driven to the bigger, better, faster, more, means we can sometimes forget to take the time to think about who we are and what we have – and to be accordingly grateful and content.

---

1   Brené Brown, *The Gifts of Imperfection: Let Go of Who You Think You're Supposed to Be and Embrace Who You Are* (Center City, MN: Hazelden Publishing, 2010).

Like so many of us, especially in recent years, I have experienced some of those big life-changing events. While they were often the most painful and bleak of times, they have undoubtedly been some of the best in terms of forcing me to think about who I really am and what I really want out of life. By reflecting on an awful time, I have made of it a lighthouse to guide me through future storms.

Undertaking self-reflection properly means it has to be rooted in honesty with ourselves. When people are asked to describe themselves in five words, they are more often than not positive and affirmative. Of course, it's always good to acknowledge the many great qualities we have, but it's also crucial to admit to those which could be seen as less positive. Authenticity is important in education, as it is in all walks of life, and it is something that comes from knowing ourselves and then working hard to know ourselves even better.

Because we don't remain static, knowing ourselves is an ongoing journey.

Why, then, do I always ask these all-important questions up front in my work? Fundamentally, it's to spark the initial thinking process needed for great coaching. The relationship between coach and client is anchored by trust, openness, confidentiality, courage and not being judgemental. By taking time to think about who we are in our personal and professional lives, we can start to make links and see any misalignment. Then, by knowing who we really are, we have the opportunity to think about what we're doing and ask questions that dig a little deeper (sometimes so deeply it can hurt). For example, do our personal values align with our professional role and also with the organisation we work for? If this is an easy yes, then you will often find yourself in the 'flow'. Working for an organisation where we buy in fully is a magical place to be. When our values and beliefs are congruent with those we work with, we can be our authentic, honest, emancipated selves.

For some, however, this enchanted workplace still eludes them and it is not a nice place to be. I should know. My thinking around authenticity and values really started in 2019. I was in work and in crisis and my mental health was being negatively affected every day I worked at this place. I am not blaming them; others were very happy there. There was simply a misalignment between me and the organisation I was working for. Something had to give and it looked like it was going to be me.

I made the decision to leave my post without a new one to go to. Scary, but liberating. I took the time to rediscover myself, to talk to people, to share and to feel – whether that was sadness, anger, disappointment or even relief. Such acute moments can also bring a much-needed clarity and purpose to life. I considered what I *could* do and what I really *wanted* to do, and wondered how I could use my experiences to support others. And then did it.

I am still on my journey, of course. I am still figuring out who I am and this will continue. We're only ever complete at the end, after all. And that's OK. Every day brings something new which causes me to think, and if I think, therefore I exist, to borrow a phrase.

So, let me ask you – who are you?

What is your immediate response? What would you say after 30 minutes of reflection? What if I asked you again tomorrow? Taking the time to think it through helps you be brave, more honest, more in control. Time and honesty give us the opportunity to make changes, to develop and then to celebrate our growth.

Let me leave with you one more question – what does this all mean in a world of social media? Is our online self – with our ability to present ourselves to the world through a carefully curated sequence of memes, quotes, photos and specially selected engagement – a less or a more authentic version of us? I still don't know. What I do know is that authenticity comes from living out our values on a daily basis regardless of who is watching or reading. So, try this: look at a social media timeline of yours – Twitter, for example – and then imagine it being printed and read out by a family member or colleague as your eulogy. Mine? Loved food, pets and coaching. Nothing really profound perhaps, but then my husband does describe me as one of the simpler carbohydrates.

Take some time to think about your answers to the question 'Who am I?' and start the process of exploring, understanding and living your values authentically. There's no self-indulgence or navel-gazing here, just an opportunity to be honest with yourself. In so doing, you get to explore what you want for yourself and for others and the important differences these discoveries can bring.

The answer to the question is within you. You just have to find it.

Matt Dechaine is a leadership coach, coaching head teachers along with supporting leadership teams. He was the head teacher of a primary school; following headship, he moved into international development. Since becoming self-employed in 2019, he has built a business supporting leaders, schools and organisations through one-to-one coaching, action learning and building authentic coaching cultures.

Chapter 23

The Joy of Mentoring

Lizana Oberholzer

The Igbo and Yoruba proverb 'It takes a village to raise a child' also rings true when we think about supporting colleagues new to the profession. Developing a teacher is something the whole school can play a part in. The new teacher may have a dedicated mentor, but anyone and everyone who is acting to support a colleague, however small those acts may be, is a mentor. This includes all the tiny voices out there.

I have always loved mentoring – an activity that can be simply defined as 'guiding' and 'giving advice'. Sometimes mentoring draws on specific skills from coaching, such as questioning and active listening, but throughout the conversations you are seeking to help the mentee on their professional journey from 'dependence to independence'.[1] I discovered this passion for mentoring early on in my teaching career. Looking back, I noticed that my professional support was not dependent on one voice mentoring me, but many helpful colleagues who enabled me, through a joint effort of 'collaborative professionalism'[2] to find my voice and my path.

One of the most helpful bits of advice a colleague gave to me while I was training was merely a passing comment: 'Remember, no one knows that you don't know, so ask if you need help.' I found it an incredibly liberating suggestion. My initial thinking had been 'What if no one thinks I can do

---

1   Mary Connor and Julia Pokora, *Coaching and Mentoring at Work: Developing Effective Practice*, 3rd edn (London: Open University Press, 2017).
2   Eleanore Hargreaves and Luke Rolls, *Unlocking Research: Reimagining Professional Development in Schools* (Abingdon: Routledge, 2021).

this?' However, as my colleague went on to explain, we have all been in the same boat at some point; we all had to start somewhere. She reassured me that initial teacher training was just that, 'initial', and that I would need to spend many hours learning the art and craft of teaching. For that learning to happen, I would need to make mistakes, reflect on them and consider new ways to move forward – wise words I still treasure to this day, especially when there is so much pressure on new teachers to be the 'finished article' so early on in their career.

It is only now that I am able to link the theory of teaching more clearly to the practice, after many years of scaffolding and layering my own learning, as a classroom practitioner and subject expert. I continued to read, and it became part of my habits as a professional learner. I now understand that teacher development really is cumulative. We are all works in progress, which means that at no point do we need to be perfect or the finished article. We often learn, as adults, by doing – then reviewing, reflecting and thinking around the theory of our practice with 'outsight', as it has been known.[3] What is important is that we allow ourselves the space to learn and grow, and that we embrace our journey with an open mind and a 'growth mindset' – a phrase we so often use in our work with students/ learners but can find so difficult to apply to ourselves as teachers.

My experience supporting future teachers over the past 17 years also tells me that we need to be more mindful of the fact that not only do adult learners and teacher trainees have different starting points, they also learn at a different pace, influenced by the contexts they engage with during their learning. As mentors, we need to keep all these variables in mind to ensure that we can best support them and help them to find their own voice as a future teacher, and develop their confidence to flourish in the classroom.

One of the most helpful theories I know for thinking about the journey new teachers are on is called the Dreyfus model.[4] It outlines how I need to consider my journey from novice to advanced beginner to expert, and frame the journey my mentees are on in the same way in order to best support them. Just as we take the time to get to know what a new class can

---

3   Herminia Ibarra, *Act Like a Leader, Think Like a Leader* (Boston, MA: Harvard Business Review Press, 2015).

4   Hubert L. Dreyfus and Stuart E. Dreyfus, *Mind over Machine: The Power of Human Intuition and Expertise in the Age of the Computer* (New York: Free Press, 1986).

or cannot do when we first meet them, we need to make sure we are not simply expecting a new teacher to be able to teach. Initial conversations that help us better understand them and their needs are always the best starting point. By engaging in these conversations with empathy – putting ourselves in their shoes – we can come to understand their starting points and work with them to map the journey that lies ahead of them in a supportive way. Mentoring and coaching strategies can be drawn on, and it can be useful to think of them as a continuum along which we move as circumstances merit; sometimes suggesting more than asking, sometimes the reverse.

A word about expectations – there is nothing wrong with having high expectations of our future teachers; however, we also need to be realistic. They need space and time to develop, to ensure that they build strong foundations for their future practice. Helping them engage with a supportive learning community can make all the difference here. Developing a strong sense of collaborative professionalism – they are new to the team, but they are still an important part of that team – will enable them to unpack their potential most effectively.

One of the things those passing words of wisdom gave me back then was a sense of agency. It was OK to ask questions, I didn't need permission for everything and it was OK for me to make my own choices and try things out. Teaching and learning are a messy business, after all, and the drive for perfection (or 'outstanding', if you like) can get in the way of any of us achieving our potential in the classroom. We need to ensure our mentees have a sense of agency that means they will try new things, take risks and then reflect on the learning the outcomes bring.

Providing a safe space where mentees can reflect on their practice and learn from you as a mentor will make all the difference. A useful task here is to co-plan lessons with your mentee. When I did this, the mentee could ask *why* I would make certain choices and what underpinned them. During this joint planning, we would also explore some of the reading that I had done around the pedagogical choices I was making, and I would encourage my mentee to find out more. We also discussed their learning, what was covered on their course so far and how it applied to the lesson plan we were working on. In this way it brought the theory of their classroom-based training to life and I made every effort to align the work they did away from school with their in-school experience.

Above all, I wanted them to remain curious, to realise that research-informed practice was important and to grasp that there are many ways to help learners to learn. Through commitment to our own ongoing professional development, we are then best placed to respond to the ever-changing needs of our learners.

Once we had worked through a wide range of joint planning sessions, I modelled teaching the lessons, all the while moving towards the mentee taking over the planning and delivery. What always impressed me about this approach was how they started giving themselves agency, talking me through their thinking and reading. The key is to model this practice from the start. Once they are in a position to move things forward themselves, they start displaying the skills you modelled. Remember that it is especially important at this stage to encourage them not to simply copy you but to develop their own teacher voice.

Of course, the magic really starts once they start to find their feet and begin to share new learning and practice with you too. If you have taken the time and care to do your initial groundwork well enough, you will arrive at that point where they are teaching you. This is when you discover the joy of mentoring as a co-constructive process, a collaborative professional journey, where both mentor and mentee enjoy becoming increasingly creative.

I am sometimes asked why being on a journey together matters. Interestingly, and although I cannot find any specific research on this, being a mentor meant my teaching was better. By tracking student results with my mentoring timetable in one establishment over a period of time, I found that my learners' outcomes, especially my exam groups, were higher in the years when I was mentoring compared to the years when I was not involved with new teachers as much. The differences were only marginal, but there was a difference. What this suggests to me is that by being more reflective and challenging yourself more during the learning relationship with your mentee, you too are becoming a better teacher. But don't take my word for it, try it for yourself.

As a tiny voice advocating for mentoring, I want to emphasise that it is so important that we give everyone involved the time and support to enjoy the many benefits this important practice brings. When mentoring is done well, you are not only developing a fantastic future teacher who will impact positively on learners for a very long time, but potentially you might be improving your own practice in the process; you will also have modelled how to be a mentor. In this way, we hope that your mentee will then pick up the torch when they are ready and mentor others into the profession too. We stand on the shoulders of giants, and by mentoring, you become one of those giants, enabling others to continue education's important work.

Lizana Oberholzer is a senior lecturer in teacher education at the University of Wolverhampton. She is the British Educational Research Association teacher education special interest group convenor in England, BAMEed Network trustee, Chartered Management Institute fellow, Chartered College of Teaching founding fellow, principal fellow of the Higher Education Academy, CollectiveED fellow, vice chair of the Universities' Council for the Education of Teachers Continuing Professional Development Forum, and multi-academy trust director.

Chapter 24

What Do You Want to Get Out of Our Time Here Together Today?

Kate Jane

Coaching wasn't something I was aware of until one of our school governors suggested it to our senior leadership team (SLT). The coaching sessions I then undertook had such a positive impact on me, improving my self-confidence and time management, and encouraging me to incorporate gratitude into my daily life; it really felt like a turning point in my life. Since then, my interest in coaching has grown, I have completed a Postgraduate Certificate in Coaching and Mentoring, and am now, myself, a qualified coach.

Coaching has changed my way of working so much and I have not only felt the benefits of being coached but also have gained so much from coaching others. For me, as a tiny voice, it really helps when I see coaching as a 'way of being,'[1] one that you can use to build your own confidence and improve your relationships and outcomes not only with colleagues but also with the learners in your classes.

You will have heard about coaching but maybe you are not sure what it is or what's involved. Confusingly, there is no one definition in the coaching

---

1   Christian van Nieuwerburgh, *An Introduction to Coaching Skills: A Practical Guide* (Thousand Oaks, CA: Sage, 2020).

world so let's just go with my absolute favourite from a coaching textbook: 'You come with your beautiful untapped potential, to be untapped and released through coaching.'[2]

Before I take you through some ways you can tap into the power of coaching in your school, a word of warning. Coaching is a one-to-one activity. It focuses on the potential we all have to move forward on a personal level. It highlights the growth we can make as individuals, not where we fit into someone else's bigger picture. This means there can be conflict between the use of coaching in schools and the need to work towards a whole-school development plan. That said, with careful planning, coaching can be incorporated into a school development plan if we consider that individuals all have different starting points and may need to be developed in different ways.

The skills used by a coach in facilitating a coaching relationship include listening, asking powerful questions, engaging in effective conversations, paraphrasing and summarising, and giving and receiving feedback. A good coach needs to be able to build rapport and a feeling of trust with the coachee. These are precious skills that take time to develop and need to be valued in those who have them. It's important to be honest here too – not everyone has the skills or characteristics to coach. They just don't. Therefore, we need to select our coaches carefully and also make sure we allow those who are being coached to choose for themselves who they would like as their coach.

Listening

If building up your repertoire of coaching skills is of interest, a great place to start is developing your own listening skills. You'll be amazed at the positive impact this can have on your relationships in school. Sometimes it seems that we have to sound knowledgeable in meetings and other interactions by speaking; however, listening is important in strengthening relationships and really understanding an issue. Begin by considering the following:

---

2   Simon Western, *Coaching and Mentoring: A Critical Text* (Thousand Oaks, CA: Sage, 2012).

- Am I listening to reply or understand?

- Does this person want my advice or do they just want me to listen?

- Am I present and really listening to what they say?

- What is my body language saying to them?

- What is my facial expression as I listen?

- Do I have the time to listen now or should I ask this person to come back later?

We all know that we feel valued when we feel someone is taking the time to really listen to us. Listening carefully is one of the kindest things we can do for someone.

Positive regard

A coach approaches everyone with positive regard, but coaches are human too. It can be a challenge for us. Our attitude towards children's behaviour in school is changing as we increasingly understand behaviour as communication, so what if we took the same approach with our colleagues? Imagine what would happen if we approached everyone at school with positive intent. The following questions can help:

- Is their behaviour related to their self-esteem?

- Have they had difficult experiences in schools in the past?

- Am I communicating well with them?

- What are their support networks within school?

- Are they struggling? Do they need help?

- Are they tired?

- Am I envious of them?

- Do I have any unconscious bias towards them?

- What else do they have going on?

When we develop empathy for others and look towards one another with positive regard, seeing everyone as an individual with the potential to grow and contribute, we go a long way to building really positive relationships. I know it can be hard. I've been there. Stepping back to consider what is behind a particular colleague's behaviour will pay dividends, I promise.

Great coaching question I

What, I wondered, would happen if I took my new 'coaching way of being' and applied it to standard SLT activities such as book scrutinies? Could I make this routine task more of a meaningful two-way conversation? What I found was that this new approach allowed for a more personalised approach between myself and teachers, facilitating coaching conversations – starting with the books – that provided moments of reflection and supported individuals to move practice forward.

Rather than being a paper exercise as they were before and as they are in so many other schools, book scrutinies became the catalyst for a coaching conversation, one that began with the magic question (and I have no idea why I had never considered using it before!): 'What do you want to get out of our time together today?'

This question is a great starting point for guiding a session and understanding how the teacher wants to move forward. Now I wasn't doing something 'to' my colleagues, I was doing something 'with' them, with an agenda led by the teacher. So, lead with that question and then follow through with some of these suggestions:

- What happened in this lesson for Child A?
  - What impact did that have?
  - How do you know?
  - Anything else?
  - What might you have done differently?
- What are your aspirations for the child(ren) in your class with special educational needs and disabilities (SEND)?

- How would that look?

- What impact would that have on you and them?

- What could you do/try?

- What do you think needs to be in place for that to happen?

- What do you think are your next steps/actions to support the child(ren) with SEND in your class?

  - When do you plan to do that by?

The above questions are really useful, but there is one more – an appropriately tiny one that is so powerful to use at the end of any coaching conversation …

Great coaching question II

'What else?'

This is such a great question to use in various interactions within school, including our teaching. Of course, the tone of how it is delivered makes a difference and I have to take care not to sound too assertive when using it. However, sometimes when we are pushed to do our deepest thinking we can come up with our best thoughts, and this question certainly pushes us. It really encourages people to move beyond their first idea, to step outside their comfort zone and explore other avenues.

Lesson observations

Observing a lesson and simply feeding back what we have seen does not have the same effect as coaching someone after the lesson. After all, we create our best learning when we do our own thinking and formulate next steps for ourselves. I feel valued if someone gives me their time, so after an observation ensure you set aside enough time to coach them through the lesson.

It is useful to break this conversation down into three parts:

1.   What is happening now?

2.   What would you like to happen?

3.   How can you make that happen?

It is important to make sure that you are in the right frame of mind before you start this conversation. Are you relaxed? Have you set aside enough time for this? This is not about you, so you need to pause and give time for the teacher to think and answer.

A good way in is the prompt 'Tell me about your lesson today'. So much can be learned from this question – it allows the teacher to reflect upon their intentions for the lesson and to think about what went well and what went less well. The following questions are then useful prompts for each part of your subsequent conversation:

1. What is happening now?

- What went well? (This is particularly important if the teacher feels the lesson was a disaster. There are positives in even the direst of lessons.)

- What was your thinking behind doing it that way?

- What helped the successful aspects of the lesson to work so well?

- What did you do to enable them to work?

- Can you use that in any other aspects of your teaching?

- What didn't go as well as you planned?

- What else? (The golden question can be added to the end of each question.)

2. What would you like to happen?

- What would it look like if everything was going as well as you wanted it to?

- How would you feel in that lesson?
- What would other people say to you if they came into that lesson?
- What would the children be doing?
- What would the adults be doing?
- What do you need to do to make that happen?
- What else?

3. How can you make that happen?

- What do you need to do to put that in place?
- You have lots of ideas about what you want to happen. What is your first step towards that happening?
- Who can/what can help you in making that happen?
- What support do you need in making that happen?
- When do you think you can achieve this by?
- Anything else?

Throughout this conversation, it will be tempting to tell the coachee what to do or to give advice, but this is not your role as a coach. Your role is to be present, to listen and to guide. Of course, there will be times when you may need to switch into a mentoring role, but if you can stay in the role of coach, having faith in the belief that individuals can create their own solutions, the results will be so much better.

Of course, before any individual or school embarks on a more 'coaching way of being', a big question will come up – does it work? It will come as no surprise to those who are already sold on the power of coaching that there is a growing body of evidence showing that coaching can impact positively on things like teacher well-being, improving classroom practice and leadership capacity.[3]

---

3   Jonathan Supovitz, Philip Sirinides and Henry May, How principals and peers influence teaching and learning, *Educational Administration Quarterly* 46(1) (2010): 31–56; Anthony M. Grant, Suzy Green and Josephine Rynsaardt, Developmental coaching for high school teachers: executive coaching goes to school, *Consulting Psychology Journal: Practice and Research* 62(3) (2010): 151–168.

In addition, this evidence has suggested that coaching may mitigate the stress of a teacher's role, with teachers who have been coached reporting lower levels of stress and higher levels of resilience than teachers who have not participated in coaching. When the researchers compared coached groups of teachers to non-coached groups, the former reported 'reduced stress, increased resilience, and improved workplace well-being'.[4] Furthermore, the researchers found additional benefits for the coached teachers including increased goal attainment and improved relationships; both protective factors for building resilience.

Coaching can have an impact on leadership skills within schools too, with research finding that 'coaching for school leaders is vital, not only to develop individual leadership capacity, but equally as systems leaders'.[5] And the National College for School Leadership noted that the impact of coaching went further than school leadership itself, with improvements in self-confidence, the ability of teachers to learn and make improvements to their practice, development of teaching strategies and a growth in confidence in their ability to have an impact through their teaching; a study that also revealed an improvement in staff retention and renewed loyalty to the school they work in.[6]

I hope I have managed to persuade tiny voices of the power of coaching. I have found that when I adopt a 'coaching way of being', approaching my colleagues with positive intent and listening to what they say with interest, my relationships have genuinely improved. A simple starting point for all of us as tiny voices in school is to ask our colleagues, 'What do you want to get out of our time here together?' It shows care and kindness and that we are valuing everyone in our schools as individuals. In that way we are doing our bit to make sure all the tiny voices are heard.

Kate Jane is a teacher of 20 years and special needs coordinator in a large primary school in Devon. She is also a coach. She has a belief in seeing the good and positive in everyone, so incorporating coaching into her role within school is a natural thing for her to do.

---

4   Supovitz, Sirinides and May, How principals and peers influence teaching and learning.
5   Mary Devine, Raymond Meyers and Claude Houssemand, How can coaching make a positive impact within educational settings? *Procedia-Social and Behavioral Sciences* 93 (2013): 1382–1389.
6   National College for School Leadership, *Leading Coaching in Schools* (London: NCSL, 2005).

Part V
Tiny Voices Tell Their Stories

What is your educational story? Are you one of those people who knew when they were 5 years of age and teaching their teddy bears that they wanted to be a teacher when they grew up? Or were you someone who ended up in teaching after a long and winding road?

I won't tell you my whole story now – that would be another book – but I will give you a few significant moments in my journey to and through teaching. I grew up in a household hearing 'those that can, do, and those that can't, teach' a great deal from my dad. That being the case, teaching was never on the cards, even though my mum was a teacher (that is a whole other story).

I went to Queen's University, Belfast (where I am from), and took a degree in Russian language and political studies, and then found myself doing a Postgraduate Certificate in Education in secondary politics and history (you can imagine my dad's horror). In the following years, I did supply, I worked in catering, I did other jobs. Then I went back to university and did a Postgraduate Certificate in Professional Development in primary education and got a job in the school where I had done my final placement.

For 18 years I climbed the career ladder and was lucky enough to work in many different roles within schools. In 2016 I was diagnosed with cutaneous mastocytosis, then in 2018 I was diagnosed with systemic mastocytosis – this explained why I was so tired at the end of the working day. It was at this point that I decided to stop climbing and move in a slightly different direction, while remaining in education. Yes, I began to create my very own climbing wall (see Part IV).

I thought about what I loved doing, and two things came up – teaching and making a difference to other educators. So I decided to return to the classroom full time in 2019, and shortly after that I became an evidence lead educator at a local research school. I wanted to do more though, so I looked into coaching qualifications, and in November 2021 I started an apprenticeship in coaching and mentoring and a Level 5 Institute of Leadership and Management diploma in coaching. Since I started the course, I have notched up over 50 hours of coaching and I absolutely love it. I feel fulfilled with my teaching, coaching and, of course, all that I do to raise 'tiny voices'.

I recall a conversation with someone who has been teaching since 1978 in which he said that the great thing about education is that there are so many different career paths. My journey has not been straightforward, or indeed straight up, but it is my journey. In the following chapters, you will be able to read the stories of other tiny voices who want you to know that there is no right way to go about things and that we all have our own stories.

Chapter 25

Kintsugi

Caitlin Bracken

Once completed, beautiful seams of gold glint in the conspicuous cracks of ceramic wares ... This unique method celebrates each artifact's unique history by emphasizing its fractures and breaks instead of hiding or disguising them.

Kelly Richman-Abdou[1]

I have always, *always* wanted to be a teacher.

The first time I told one of my teachers that I wanted to teach too, I was 16. I hadn't completely gone quiet yet, though I was no stranger to the uncomfortable, panicky feeling of my words drying up. My GCSE history teacher, Mr M, asked me what I wanted to do when I finished school. I felt shy but drew myself up and said, 'I want to be a primary school teacher, Sir.'

I will never forget his reaction. I expected a laugh, an incredulous expression, anything to match the swirling uncertainty in my stomach when it came to my childhood aspiration. But Mr M smiled, almost proudly. 'I can really see you doing that,' he replied. I felt 12 feet tall. Someone whose

---

1   Kelly Richman-Abdou, Kintsugi: the centuries-old art of repairing broken pottery with gold, *My Modern Met* (5 March 2022). Available at: https://mymodernmet. com/kintsugi-kintsukuroi/.

opinion I respected so much could see through my quietness and could, by some miracle, see a teacher.

I am a teacher because my teachers believed in me.

My journey to realising the dream has not been a simple one. Always the quiet one, always reluctant to raise my hand and make myself the centre of attention, always the one with the cardigan sleeve she had nervously shredded, always the one at parents' evening to receive that dreaded feedback: 'Oh, she's doing so well, but she really needs to speak up more!'

The Japanese craft of *kintsugi* has inspired me so much in recent months as I look back over my struggles to become a teacher. It describes a way of repairing broken pottery with gold, making the object unique and all the more beautiful in the process. Philosophically speaking, it means treating our past as something to cherish rather than hide. Our damage makes us unique and all the more beautiful too.

In sixth form, despite being an A-grade student, I could barely answer the register, much less make the kind of extended, reasoned comments required of A-level historians. Regardless of whether I knew my teachers, or whether I was sitting beside friends I'd had since primary school, I was the same in all my subjects. My voice had slipped away, and my belief in my ability to become a teacher was slipping away with it. Generalised anxiety disorder (GAD) had crept in and effectively turned me mute.

I learned at that point that kindness is often found in the quietest actions and it was my teachers who came to my rescue. When my self-belief had reached an all-time low, the belief they had in me never once faltered. What can we all learn from such kindness?

For a start, the power of noticing.

Noticing is hugely important as a teacher, both academically and pastorally. We notice when work needs to be harder or easier; we notice when children are struggling or flying through things. We also need to notice when children are acting differently, when something's a little off. Because we're *in loco parentis*, we owe it to them to look out for them and know what's normal for them and what isn't.

Great pupil–teacher relationships make good days better and can salvage magic from the wreckage of the bad ones. I learned the hard way that when your world feels like it's falling apart, knowing that at least one teacher has your back can make all the difference. Thank you, Mr M. Thank you, Madame K, too.

Madame K was my brilliant GCSE French teacher. She tamed our rowdy class of 30 by believing in us with every fibre of her being, turning us eventually into a group of half-decent linguists. She called us 'la crème de la crème' when she was teaching us advanced grammar or turns of phrase that reached beyond the syllabus.[2] She called us collectively her 'petits choux-fleurs' and individual terms of genuine affection such as 'sweet one' or 'ma puce', and the improbably endearing 'dollyflops'. Even pushing 16, we only ever took her words as labels of endearment, and we wore them with pride. I loved being in her class, and my passion for languages and burning desire for every pupil now in my care to feel special, come from her.

My love of languages that Madame K inspired prompted me to go on and take French at A level. The thing is, Madame K died on Remembrance Day in my final year in sixth form and, although my anxiety was pretty bad already, it all became a lot worse after that.

It was difficult to avoid speaking in small sixth-form classes to begin with, but it was impossible to hide in a French class of just five, with a grade that depended upon a speaking component. At times, my anxiety meant I could barely speak in English on a one-to-one basis, so you can imagine the state I was in when I had to speak in front of people in another language, all while drowning in revision and applying for a university course for which I definitely didn't think I was good enough. I was quietly also grieving for Madame K.

Why did I stick at it? Enter Mr G.

'The growing good of the world is partly dependent on unhistoric acts', wrote George Eliot.[3] Mr G's constant stream of unhistoric acts made a momentous difference to me. He gave me so much of his time, trying to help. It is only since becoming a teacher myself and knowing how precious

---

2   At 23, I now understand her literary reference!
3   George Eliot, *Middlemarch* (Edinburgh: William Blackwood and Sons, 1872).

our time is that I've fully understood how caring and generous he truly was.

One of the most impactful steps you can take to nurture academic or pastoral development is to make yourself available to your pupils. Every young person deserves to be heard, from the Reception child who wants a hug when he's told you about his bad dream last night, to the sixth-former drowning in coursework, anxiety, revision and grief. If a pupil trusts you enough to share with you that they are struggling, it may be a privilege they have not afforded to anyone else. There are never enough hours in a day, I know, but please make the time for those who need you.

I wouldn't be a teacher at all, never mind the determined one that I am, if I hadn't had Mr G backing me up all the way. When someone can tell you're going to panic before you know it yourself, that's a superpower in my book (and I know Mr G would be embarrassed at being thought of as a superhero!).

*

Sixth-form life was pretty grim but I made it. I might have been in several broken and reassembled pieces, but I was joined together with fresh gold and heading for university to train as a teacher. Of course, I took my GAD with me, but was relieved to find kindred spirits in both my classmates and my tutors; people who saw past my quietness. There were some dark days during my 3 years of teacher training, and my first year as a teacher – still with GAD, still determined to teach and now with an attack of imposter syndrome – was made all the worse by the COVID-19 pandemic. Turns out it's quite hard to feel like a teacher when your medium is reduced to PowerPoints, video clips and Word documents set from the desk in the corner of your bedroom. You don't need me to tell you how easy it was to feel anxious and isolated at that awful time, and by the end of that year there was little left of the gold that had filled the scars of anxieties past. I felt shattered, broken down to tiny pieces that seemed they would never fit together again to resemble the Miss Bracken who had started her career the previous September.

*

I'm not the same teacher, or even the same woman, that I was that summer. This forced break in my classroom practice gave me so much time to reflect – after all, as a chronic overthinker, I'm good at this. But this reflection has changed my outlook on certain areas of my teaching and my teacher persona that I really look forward to applying for real. For example, if you aren't inclined naturally to open up, it can be difficult to start doing so, but my greatest tip for any teacher (especially a quiet one, or one coming out of some challenging experiences) is to find your 'we'. So much personal and professional growth can come from sharing with colleagues who you trust. There is an impossible balance to be struck, of course, but allowing yourself to be vulnerable and reaching out for help can lead to huge development in the long term. Taking the brave step to admit my vulnerability, and ask for help, led to guidance and support that I deeply valued.

If we are honest, we know we're all damaged in one way or another, yet we all have the capacity to put ourselves back together with gold *kintsugi* style and be better than before. We just have to be brave enough to find the people who want us to succeed, like Mr M and Mr G and dear Madame K. Their belief will carry us in the moments when we can't carry ourselves and, when the time comes, we can be that person carrying others who need help too.

Caitlin Bracken is a quiet teacher who has found her voice through blogging since a tumultuous induction year as a newly qualified teacher year in 2020. She is passionate about play in Key Stage 1 and reading for pleasure school-wide. A proud alumna of Liverpool Hope University, Caitlin is a northern girl at heart, now teaching and living in Buckinghamshire.

Chapter 26
The Short Long Way Round

Bronté Hobson-Scott

'Bronté, there are other roles in education besides teaching. Maybe one of those is right for you?'

Such words from your tutor during what you thought was going to be your teacher training come as a bit of a blow. I had always wanted to teach. Having been fortunate enough to experience great teaching, I caught a love of learning and saw the opportunities that great educators can have on a learner's outcomes. I started, therefore, with a sprint but then soon ran out steam, tripping over the loose stones and getting lost in the woods. Benched for lack of competence (I mean 'confidence'), I moved to the near-by town of learning support and watched the rest of the student teachers on my course race to the finish with a bittersweet smile.

Now what?

When good advice stops stinging, it starts to sink in. I was on a different path now but it was still a path. I volunteered in any school that would have me, and I actually enjoyed working in different settings and areas. It turns out I had a knack for spotting and then helping the students who struggled quietly. But volunteering doesn't pay the bills, so I applied to be a teaching assistant (TA). Maybe this was my road to a classroom of my own? My sprint became a marathon. I was going to have to take the long way round.

I worked my way around the TA world – secondary, primary and a bit of alternative provision – before I settled in a school that seemed to see something in me. I'd found the place to rest my pencil case and readied myself to ensure the long way round was as short as possible.

My natural ability with vulnerable and struggling students (also on their own marathon) really came to the fore now. Working with them became a large part of my role and students who had difficulties accessing their learning for any number of reasons became my speciality. Seeing what these children could achieve with specialist support was heart-warming, and building relationships and collecting resources to help these children avoid falling through the net became something I was good at. It was something I loved to do too.

But my childhood dream was always to be a teacher. I realised that I had nearly given up on that dream, which was annoying. It wasn't as though I'd wanted to be a pop star or prime minister or Phoebe from *Friends*. I just wanted to teach; it shouldn't have been this hard.

My marathon had turned into a load of squiggly lines on a map, like someone who's been on a really long run, stopped for a few cups of tea and gone on a day trip to Blackpool in the fog. I was having a great time, but I had lost my way.

But through the mist I could make out the vague outline of what Miss Hobson-Scott 'the teacher' might look like. Whole-class teaching was no longer filling me with dread, and I threw myself into setting up provisions and planning the most extravagant of lessons (before learning to plan practical and nice ones because extravagant is hard work and expensive and quite frankly unsustainable).

I am starting to value the steady jog now – the short long way round. I know where I want to be. I'm unwavering in my determination to get there but I'm happy to have taken my time. Each fork in the road I took meant I learned so much that would serve me in good stead as a class teacher and benefit the children in my care. Each term that passes when I haven't yet applied for accreditation is a term that I have spent learning, listening and educationally 'carb-loading' for that sprint to the finish line that I know I will complete.

If you aren't quite where you (or your mum) thought you'd be by now, this is my advice – get as much experience as you can. Say yes to everything, do things you haven't done before and explore other roles and responsibilities in education. In this way, one day, you and your students will reap so many rewards from your short long way round.

Bronté Hobson-Scott BSc, a perpetual TA-turned-graduate co-teacher from Yorkshire, is passionate about the slow pursuit of adding strings to her bow in her journey towards qualified teacher status.

Chapter 27

Outside Noise

Lucy Griffiths

At the time of writing this, I am just about to start my 20th year in the classroom. I currently teach in a small school with 210 children and seven lovely teachers, but this tiny voice has a big secret and I think it's time to get it off my chest and finally come clean. You see, when I say, 'currently teach', what I really mean is 'have always taught'. That's right, I have only ever worked in one school: this one. For 19 years. Before you judge me, tell me I must be 'stagnant', that I should be 'climbing the ladder' or 'developing myself' in other ways, let me give you eight good reasons why I have stayed put:

1. I'm happy there.

2. I earn good money – not the be-all and end-all but it helps.

3. I love the school.

4. I believe totally in the school ethos.

5. The staff are my friends.

6. Some of the staff are my best friends.

7. At the risk of sounding cheesy, we are like a family.

8. Did I mention I am happy there?

The newest member of our teaching family has been here for 'just' 5 years and you might think of it like an educational Bermuda Triangle – once you get in, you can't get out.[1] I like to think of it as more of a case of 'once you find your tribe, you stay'. Don't get me wrong, we've been through some tough times. I can get really irritated and I've contemplated leaving on a few occasions, but my heart is in my school and the school is a huge part of my life.

Of course, I nearly left a few years ago. My head teacher kept telling me I needed to move on, to grow, that I should go and experience another school as a deputy head. My parents, best friends and husband were all telling me the same thing. I began to listen to all that outside noise, starting to feel guilty and less worthy by having stayed put all these years. I applied for a deputy headship in another school because, well, that's what you're supposed to do, isn't it?

I didn't get the job. I went through the whole application and interview process, of course, and the head teacher at the other school was absolutely lovely. She said I would make a great deputy but could tell that I didn't want the job. She was right. I just wanted to go 'home'. I returned to my school knowing that it was the right place for me. My head teacher was, of course, thrilled and gave me more responsibility, so everybody wins.

So that's my guilty tiny secret. I've been where I am for years and I am happy. Except, I have another secret to share. I have been a Year 5 class teacher for many years too. Hear me out! I still get the opportunity to teach other classes every week and probably teach more children than most. In my school, on a set day every week, the junior children move around the teachers to be taught the foundation subjects. It's a noisy, busy, open-plan school where we don't follow a normal timetable, so people who come to our school find it very hard to understand how we teach the way we teach. We dress up in role a lot. We play lots of games. We use fun resources and the children are really active in their learning. I also get the joy of teaching reception on Fridays. Being in a small, innovative, creative primary school also has so many benefits because of the size of the community. We know *all* the children really well and enjoy great relationships with all the parents and carers and the wider community too.

---

1   Two members of staff left recently to take up other jobs that they thought would be less stressful. Both returned within months because they missed us.

So no, I'm not going anywhere. And if you don't want to, you don't have to either. Don't let outside noise guide what you do with your career. If you are happy, that's OK. That's plenty. There are enough unhappy teachers out there, after all. I'm not saying don't go for other jobs but, if you find a school where you are happy and you are excited to be there and you are making a difference and you miss your 'family' when you're not with them, then it's OK. Stay.

Lucy Griffiths is in her 20th year of teaching. She is passionate about reading for pleasure and creative writing, and is in charge of pastoral care and well-being at her school. Lucy has written two books – Are We There Yet? and The Snowman and The Swallow. She is also a cold-water swimmer in her spare time.

Chapter 28
Mostly Stuck

Emma Platt

'Multiple sclerosis' (MS) – to hear those two words at 18 years old changed my life.

I was diagnosed with MS at 18, meaning I've had it for a quarter of a century, probably longer. I'm quite open about it, but I'm aware that when I mention those two words, the vacant look on people's faces means they don't know what it is. Unfortunately, people see the label and not me; let's face it, people fear the unknown.

For those of you who haven't heard of MS, I'll explain a bit about it. A substance called myelin protects the nerve fibres in our central nervous system and helps messages travel quickly and smoothly between the brain and the rest of the body. With MS, your immune system, which normally helps to fight off infections, mistakes myelin for a foreign body and attacks it. This damages the myelin and strips it off the nerve fibres, either slightly or completely, leaving scars known as lesions or plaques. This damage disrupts messages travelling along nerve fibres – they can slow down, become distorted or not get through at all. As well as losing the myelin, there can sometimes be damage to the actual nerve fibres too. It's this nerve damage that can cause more serious issues over time.

More than 130,000 people in the UK have MS. Women are three times as likely to get it than men, and no two people's symptoms are the same. There are different types of MS – primary progressive MS (PPMS), secondary progressive MS (SPMS) and relapsing, remitting MS (RRMS). I have RRMS, which means I am well for much of the time but then will have attacks of new and old symptoms. This is called a relapse. Around 85% of people with MS are diagnosed with RRMS. This means that the symptoms enter a period of remission and go away completely. To look at me, you wouldn't know any different; you'll never see me in high heels though!

Do I let it get in the way of me living my life? Absolutely not. I refuse to let that happen. My attendance at work is excellent and I have never had time off due to MS.

I am married with two amazing children aged 4 and 9. I work full time; I've been a successful assistant head teacher for 7 years. I've travelled the world – skiing in Vermont, taking 42 secondary school pupils to the top of the Empire State Building, school trips to Japan, road trips to California and New Orleans, holidays to Mexico and many more. The point I'm trying to make is, MS doesn't hold me back. I just wish people would see past the label!

I want to further my career and become a deputy head teacher, but at times I think people see the letters MS on an application form and panic. I dread filling in the 'medical condition' section. Teaching application forms often have a 'Recruitment and monitoring' section, which specifically asks whether the applicant considers themselves to be disabled, with 'Yes' or 'No' tick boxes, alongside an explanation that the legal definition of disability is: 'a physical or mental impairment which has a substantial and long-term adverse effect on a person's ability to carry out normal day-to-day activities'. Some of these forms even state: 'Some specific conditions deemed to be disabilities include HIV, cancer, multiple sclerosis and severe disfigurements.'

So, do I class myself as having a disability? I am not registered disabled, so why is MS even a box I have to tick on a job application form?

I know employers need to know whether I am suitable to be employed at their school, and I understand there may be worries, particularly over attendance (although my attendance is excellent!). I'm caught in a catch-22. Yes, I know schools say they will interview you as long as you meet the 'essential criteria of the employee specification', but funnily enough, if I do mention my MS, I don't get an interview and if I neglect to mention it, I get that interview. Go figure.

If I do get an interview, at what point do I drop my MS into the conversation? Do I mention it at the informal phone-call stage and risk not getting a face-to-face interview or, even worse, a 'pity interview'? Do I wait until day two of a deputy head teacher interview process, have a quiet word with the head and watch the job go to the 'safe option'? Do I wait until I get the job, then just, you know, let them know? Or am I open and honest from the start and watch that dream job just evaporate?

What would you do?

I find myself feeling **M**ostly **S**tuck and trying to **M**ake **S**ense of the next part of my career journey; at the time of writing, I still haven't landed that deputy head teacher position, despite several interviews. Perhaps it is to do with the MS, or perhaps I'm just no good at interviews!

Just because somebody has an 'invisible' condition, it does not mean they can't do their job. Just because somebody has an 'invisible' condition, it does not mean they shouldn't be given a chance. So, if you are ever involved in the shortlisting process and see that box ticked on an application form, **M**ake **S**ure you look at the person before you discount them, because it might just be the best appointment you've made.

Emma Platt has been a teacher for 21 years, and is currently an assistant head teacher and English teacher at a secondary high school in Manchester. She is the lead for teaching and learning, and curriculum standards. Emma has been happily married for 13 years and is a mum to two beautiful daughters.

Chapter 29

Coming into Education Later in Life

Nazia Dar

The year was 2011. I was a mother to a 6-year-old and a 1-year-old, and I had just hit 40. It was time to quit my job in finance and embark on a teaching career.

Overwhelmed pretty much describes my Postgraduate Certificate in Education experience: pedagogy, phonics, syntax, qualified teacher status, assessment for learning, every child matters, Vygotsky, Piaget, Bruner, Bloom. I was out of my depth.

Placements were hard. I picked up quickly that you were lucky to be on a placement. It seemed like the school was doing the university a favour, so I felt the need to bend over backwards to make the school happy and ensure the university didn't lose the place. I had always assumed the school was there to help the student, not the other way round.

In my first placement, during one observation, I had the head, the deputy head and my mentor sitting in three chairs at the front of my class. With clipboards. In my second, I was paired with a disgruntled teacher who was leaving. I taught her class for her all day every day. She could not be bothered to mentor me.

The best placement I had was in a pupil referral unit for 3 weeks. It was hard but I felt nurtured and supported. I fell in love with the support

161

teaching we offered to those hard-to-reach pupils – the children who really needed us most.

When my PGCE ended, I stopped. I needed to re-evaluate what I wanted from my extreme career change. I did supply teaching, and this is where I came in to my own. I travelled from school to school and saw what so many different schools were like. I started to enjoy meeting other teachers. I learned that those PGCE placements were not normal. They shouldn't have had to be so hard after all.

In January 2013 I started my newly qualified teacher (NQT) year. In the end I spent 2 years as an NQT as I made the decision to go down to one day a week in my final term – a choice I do not regret. It was the right thing to do for me and my family at the time.

During my NQT years I learned so much. The biggest lesson I learned was from my head. During an observation she said: 'This is your class. You are responsible for them. If you are given plans that you think will not benefit your children, it is up to you to adapt them to what your children need. Take risks and, most of all, enjoy teaching.'

I ended up staying in that school for 6 years. I learned so much from the amazing teachers who mentored me and from such a supportive senior leadership team. The school was rated 'Requires improvement' when I joined. They became an academy 2 years later and went on to be 'Good' in their next Ofsted inspection.

Six years later, I had itchy feet. I wanted to see what other schools were like. I was scared to move as I was in my comfort zone but, for someone like me, this meant I had to move. But so many doubts! What if I didn't even get shortlisted for an interview? What if I went for an interview and I didn't get the job? What if the school I went to was awful? However, I knew that if I didn't make this move, I'd end up in my school at the time for my whole teaching career, and I needed a change. I needed to change. I needed to stand on my own two feet and see what I could offer another school from all that I had learned in the school I was in. And I wanted to see what I could learn from outside the walls of the academy.

So, in July 2018, I left.

I began at a new school in September 2018. Thanks to all I had learned in my previous school and my mentors who had pushed me to be the best for the children in my care, I knew I could stand on my own two feet now.

Three years later, I am still as passionate about teaching as I was in my previous school. I have been fortunate enough to work with a head teacher who has let me trial new educational concepts and listened to my vision for teaching and learning. But then the COVID-19 pandemic arrived. The well-being of children and staff, not to mention the hit to the school budget, mean those plans are on hold, for now.

So where does that leave me? I am moving to Key Stage 1, back out of my comfort zone and challenged once again. I am excited. And yes, as an experienced teacher, I am still scared.

What have I learned from my journey so far? There will be tears and moments of doubt. There will be anger, rage and, in my case, much stomping of feet. Throughout your teaching career, there will be days when you will want to give up. (My latest one was only this year.) There will be days when you hate everyone and everything. There will be times when someone decides to take credit for your ideas. These days come. And they will go.

But remember, there will be days when you are floating on air because you made a difference to one child's life. There will be days when a parent thanks you for caring about their child. There will be days when you love everyone and everything about your life and teaching. There will be days when you are given credit for your ideas. These days come. And they too will go.

Through it all, never forget the essence of why you came into teaching. My motivation was to change lives and to ensure that all children received the best education I could give them.

My future? I have no idea what will happen. However, I will continue to take one step at a time and hope that the passion I feel today will accompany me throughout the journey.

Nazia Dar started teaching in 2011, after a career in finance, and is currently a class teacher based in an inner-London school. She is passionate about children reading quality books that promote diversity in the world to address the inequalities in society.

Chapter 30
Less Why, More How!

Rebecca Waker

You know those people who go into teaching because they had this amazing teacher who inspired them and they thought, 'When I grow up, I want to be like you'? Or the ones who had such a lousy time at school themselves, they commit from a young age that, 'When I grow up, I'm going to be a teacher and make sure no one suffers like I did'? Or the ones who come from a teaching dynasty and say, 'When I grow up, I'm going to be like my parents and their parents before them'? Or the ones who say, 'I don't want to grow up. I'm going into teaching!'?

Well, I was none of these.

I just thought I might be OK at it and decided I'd give it a go. Seven years later and I'm still here, so I guess it wasn't the worst decision ever. It's quite easy to feel guilty or that something is wrong with you when you don't have a great 'why' story to share in the staffroom or at a conference, so how about celebrating those with a 'how' story as well? I'm not here to be inspirational. I just want to know all I can about how learning works. A little less 'why' and a lot more 'how'.

From early on, the 'how' was something I was really interested in. When others were complaining about their Postgraduate Certificate in Education assignments, I was quite enjoying them. I always wanted to read more, know more, dig a little deeper. The trouble is, when you're *that* person, you can feel like the odd one out – at least I certainly did. Starting my master's in education at the end of my first year as a qualified teacher probably didn't help my cause!

On top of that, as soon as I heard about the Chartered College of Teaching, I knew it was something I wanted to be involved with. The idea of a body that was not only bringing teachers together for professional connection and support, but also making research evidence accessible to help us improve practice seemed right up my street. Being member 400-and-something shows I was among the first to sign up. I then felt that my edu-nerd status was really made official when I joined the pilot for the Chartered Teacher programme. I was finally surrounded by like-minded teachers who also were fascinated by the 'how' of education.

So, this tiny voice is saying, 'Edu-nerds of the world, unite!' You are not alone, so reach out and make connections and find us – we are there. Social media is your friend here, especially if you are feeling a little isolated in your department or school. There are a number of platforms you can use, but Twitter is the best place to start. Forget the tittle-tattle and the tribes and the egos (use the 'block' and 'mute' functions at will!) and get yourself a cool network of like-minded edu-tweeps who are keen to learn and share. You'll find blogs to read, podcasts to listen to and many organised chats to join in with. Social media means continuing professional development is at your fingertips, whether you are looking for formal courses to attend – online or in the real world – or just to enjoy the informal nature of many of the chats and threads. Note that it's not all about sharing your resources and who's got the biggest PowerPoint. Just join in, be online and behave – be a cheerleader not a critic.

What's more, after dipping your edu-nerd toes in the water by reading, listening and attending, you may well choose to make your own tiny voice heard by being the one writing, recording and speaking. And if those opportunities don't come to you, you're free to create them for yourself.

Communities exist in the real world too, so make sure you are using your online network to help build a real-life one as well, whether that's groups such as subject associations or year-group or phase networks. And of course, there is the Chartered College of Teaching where all the cool teachers hang out.

There is no need to suffer if you are, like me, the only edu-nerd in the school. There are a whole host of ways to unite with others like you, and who knows? It could eventually lead to more opportunities, or finding the right school or role later down the line. Just keep being a practitioner who isn't dazzled by the 'why' but is definitely interested in the 'how', and wear that edu-nerd badge with pride.

Rebecca Waker is a lead practitioner for modern foreign languages at the Cornelius Vermuyden School in Essex. She founded #MFLChat on Twitter and has a podcast discussing educational reading and its application to practice called From Page to Practice.

Chapter 31

Why Dyslexic People Make Great Teachers

Gemma Clark

We require people with a unique mind, so only dyslexics (like Steve) should apply.

Recruitment advert, the Garage

The above is a line from a famous recruitment ad run by a marketing company in 2016.[1] The 'Steve' they are referring to is, of course, Steve Jobs.

What the marketing firm recognised is what others in the world of work, from Virgin and Microsoft to Facebook and even Government Communications Headquarters, have also recognised – people with dyslexia think differently, and that's a good thing.[2]

---

1   Matthew Weaver, Marketing firm posts 'only dyslexics need apply' job advert, *The Guardian* (11 February 2016). Available at: https://www.theguardian.com/society/2016/feb/11/job-advertisement-uk-thinktank-recruit-dyslexics-only-steve-jobs-garage.

2   EY, *The Value of Dyslexia: Dyslexic Capability and Organisations of the Future* (2019). Available at: https://assets.ey.com/content/dam/ey-sites/ey-com/en_uk/topics/diversity/ey-the-value-of-dyslexia-dyslexic-capability-and-organisations-of-the-future.pdf.

It is estimated that one in ten people have dyslexia;[3] therefore, most classrooms will have dyslexic learners. Dyslexic children often feel 'stupid', and it is important they are empowered with an understanding of their neurological difference by seeing 'people like them' in their school communities and in popular culture, as well as being successful as a sought-after commodity in the world of work. Knowing dyslexic adults who have succeeded and seeing them being positive about their dyslexia can make such a difference for bolstering the self-esteem and self-belief of children and young people who spend so much time feeling just plain dumb.

People like me.

My dyslexia was not diagnosed until my early 30s, during my teacher training, and even this happened by chance. One day, waiting outside the lecture hall, I was chatting with another student about how I was finding the course reading a real challenge. I mentioned how I often have to read and re-read journal articles to properly understand them. My fellow student recognised this in herself and asked me, 'Are you dyslexic too?' I reassured her that I wasn't and she looked at me closely and said, 'Are you sure? Have you ever been assessed?' I hadn't.

I went to student disability services at the university, who arranged an appointment with an educational psychologist. It didn't take long for me to be diagnosed with dyslexia.

It was a shock and a relief. I had assumed I was just a slower learner, that my struggles through school and university and now into teacher training were, well, just me. By the age of 17 when I started university (not an uncommon age to start in Scotland), I had taught myself various strategies to compensate for my difficulty. However, I just thought having to pull regular all-nighters and read journal articles several times in order to understand them was just the way it was, just the way I was.

I had always known, deep down as a young child, there was something different about me. I loved to read but really struggled as soon as I was given one of those dreaded comprehension tasks. My reading out loud would sound great, even though I had no idea what I had just read. At secondary school I realised that I was unable to read if there was any noise in the class and used to ask if I could take my books out to the corridor. At primary

---

3   See https://www.nhs.uk/conditions/dyslexia/.

school I was frequently shouted at for being 'lazy' and 'refusing to learn' my times tables despite relentless late nights spent trying to commit them to memory. They never seemed to stick, no matter what I did.

My dyslexia is considered 'mild', so imagine the struggles of children who have more pronounced dyslexia – struggles with trying to succeed academically in a world that seems set up to make them look stupid, struggles with their sense of worth and ability. This is why early diagnosis of dyslexia is very important for a young person's mental health. As it did for me with my later diagnosis, it helps to explain why we find some things harder than other people. It is of immense importance for a child to understand that they are not 'stupid' but that they have a brain that works in a different (and potentially so much more creative and useful) way.

I don't blame teachers for having become frustrated with me, despite some pretty awful memories, and for not picking up on my difficulty. The dyslexia training that teachers receive is still far from adequate today and I certainly received very little dyslexia training at university. My best continuing professional development in this area has been my lived experience, along with a student placement alongside a teacher who had undertaken a lot of extra training on the topic.[4]

Sadly, as a new teacher, I experienced prejudice at work, right from the outset. I had attended a growth mindset training session early in my career which had advocated sharing your own struggles in learning with children in order to inspire them and encourage resilience. Inspired myself, I floated the idea of sharing my dyslexia with my class, only to be told not to as 'Parents will think you are illiterate and complain about you.'

I was shocked. More than that, I was deeply hurt. If these attitudes can be so painful to a grown adult, imagine the stigma a dyslexic child will feel. Always remember that children are intuitive; they pick up on your real attitudes and what you think about their abilities, or otherwise. I have also heard staff say there is no point screening children who are showing signs of dyslexia but 'coping'. I was the child who 'coped' (and pretty well, if I may say so) but I still had struggles and internal battles and felt unnecessarily stupid for so much of the time.

---

4   This teacher was the one who also pointed out that my dyslexia, not stupidity, was to blame for my poor sense of direction.

Now, as a more experienced teacher, I no longer seek permission to be myself with my children. (I have also worked with head teachers who have been very supportive of me sharing my diagnosis with my class.) As a new teacher, I would ensure I had times tables answers to hand and would rehearse texts before I read them out loud to a class. However, I have since abandoned these practices. The children know that I use the same skip counting strategy for times tables that I teach them if they are struggling to memorise them. I no longer worry if I have trouble with words while reading out loud. The children understand that sometimes I stumble or accidentally misread things or skip words. If it is OK for me to do this, it makes it OK for them to do it too. I would go so far as to say that sharing my dyslexia with my class has been one of the best things that I have done to raise academic attainment and model resilience and a growth mindset. I always tell children, 'It's OK to be unsure about spelling, I always need to check too' or, 'If you need extra time for your reading task, that's OK. I take longer to do these things too.'

I have also learned that this openness about my dyslexia makes it safe for children with other differences and disabilities to be themselves too. I have had several classes over the years where children who are autistic or who have attention deficit hyperactivity disorder (ADHD) have also begun to talk openly about it with their classmates. This always makes the class feel more inclusive. Diversity is healthy, after all. I have observed the wonderful learning opportunities for the whole class when children say things like, 'I have ADHD and sometimes I need to move around' or, 'Autism is my superpower and sometimes I need a quiet place to go to.' It is amazing how supportive and accepting neurotypical children can be when, given the opportunity to learn about and understand their neurodiverse classmates.

A great starting point in schools is to make sure we have dyslexic teachers, like me, on the staff. One of the most important benefits they bring is that we understand children's struggles in learning. Dyslexic people instinctively find strategies that make our lives easier and we can then share these with our pupils. Often what helps me, helps dyslexic learners (and what helps dyslexic learners, helps all learners).

That said, teaching itself is a highly bureaucratic profession; an aspect of the job that is not dyslexia friendly. How can we tackle this and encourage more dyslexic people into the profession? While I personally prefer to call myself 'neurodiverse', most countries have disability laws which protect dyslexic people from discrimination and require 'reasonable adjustments' to be made at work. These could include parent phone calls instead of written reports or simplified (less wordy!) planning documents. It shouldn't matter what other teachers are doing. A person who requires wheelchair access should not have to justify their adaptation and neither should dyslexic teachers.

If you are a dyslexic teacher, or if you are dyslexic and considering becoming a teacher, ask for dyslexia-friendly documents and policies or audio versions of these. If your employer does not have them, ask why not. Consider approaching human resources or your trade union if you feel you are not being treated fairly and supported adequately.

Let me suggest one other area where our superpower can be put to great use and benefit everyone – planning. After all, one of the talents that the companies I mentioned at the beginning of my chapter want from dyslexic people is our ability to simplify unnecessarily complicated things. As Chris Arnold, the man behind that famous dyslexia ad, says, 'If you wanted to assemble the world's best choir you'd want great singers, not tone-deaf ones. We are simply looking for the best innovative thinkers and they are usually dyslexics.'[5] So, put us in charge of creating school plans and imagine how much quicker and less cluttered life would be for all teachers. Dyslexic teachers could be the answer to teacher workload that we have all been looking for.

Gemma Clark is a dyslexic psychology graduate and primary school teacher from Scotland. She is passionate about inclusive education and health and well-being. She is also a Massage in Schools instructor and children and family yoga instructor. She believes in taking a well-being-focused and holistic approach to teaching children.

---

5   Weaver, Marketing firm posts 'only dyslexics need apply' job advert.

Chapter 32
The Wisdom of Talking Heads

Oliver Wright

All of the best teachers I've ever worked with have underestimated their impact and overestimated their shortcomings.

I recently tweeted this to a teacher who I also consider a good friend. They were having one of those moments of self-doubt, familiar to everyone doing an important job that they care deeply about, and it got me thinking.

Many of us struggle with a sense of not being worthy, of not being good enough, which means we also struggle with a sense of belonging. After all, who would want us if we're not that good? Then the tiny voices like us end up simply looking mutely at those with the biggest voices who always seem to have something important to say about what they've done, where they've been and who they are. It's one of the dangers of social media, as we know.

Fortunately, there are spaces, like this book, where the smaller voices can get themselves out there and I've been fortunate to present a radio show called *Talking Heads* on @TeacherHugRadio. It's a simple concept – just an open-ended, cosy chat with a head teacher. We explore how they got into teaching, how they progressed into leadership, what drives them and what they're up to now. I'm not looking for anything sensational or controversial, just a chance for them to reflect and share their wisdom.

It's fascinating to observe how we have all been shaped by our experiences and the people around us. It's equally fascinating to see the way we have all 'paid this forward' and the effect this generosity has had on the children we work with.

I have interviewed many heads for the programme – some you may have heard of, many you won't. They have all had wonderful nuggets of wisdom to share, regardless of how big their voices are in the wider world. So, what have I learned from these amazing conversations? Here are my top ten insights, starting with the most important:

1. Everyone has something to say, something to add to the general pool of professional wisdom – not just the noisy ones. You have something to add too.

2. Find a position and a school that are a good fit for you. Schools and roles are massively varied and it's important to be in an environment where you're comfortable being you. And those around you are comfortable with you being you too. You also need to be doing a job that you're comfortable in. Leading maths may look good on your CV, but if it's not you then you're unlikely to be the best at it. Taking a lead in another area of school life may be a much better fit and you'll be much happier and more effective into the bargain. The same is true for the age range or phase you work with. If you're on this planet to be an early years teacher, then do that and do it to the best of your ability. No good will come from trying to squeeze yourself into the guise of a Year 6 teacher.

3. Look for the best fit, not the perfect one. Perfection rarely exists in any area of life and its pursuit can be a dangerous endeavour. Look for somewhere that is relatively well aligned with your values and outlook, and accept that such a good fit is good enough. This will make your search for a suitable position so much more likely to succeed. Being in a school or a role that is, let's say, 80% there, enables you to get off to a great start and to focus your energies more efficiently on impacting children's learning. Nowhere is perfect all the time and so often it's the attitude that you bring to your work that will make the difference anyway.

4.   You're only as good as your last class. Whatever you aspire to do or be professionally, your core purpose will always be teaching and learning. This is where your focus needs to be. This is where you will have the maximum impact on children's lives. You need to get the basics right and be a solid class teacher before you worry about taking on extra responsibilities. Once you do take on extra, never let it have a negative impact on your core purpose of teaching. You can't lead others if what is happening in your own classroom isn't up to scratch.

5.   Develop your unique strengths. Once you're a good class teacher, if you're ambitious, you need to have a key area that's your 'thing' – something that you're passionate about, that sets you apart. Then become excellent at that. Schools need a variety of key skills, so there will always something for you. If it's reading, become passionately amazing at it. If it's assessment, become indispensable with data. The joy of working in schools is that all these areas of expertise come together across a whole staff team. And your passion and skill will draw people to you. Be the sports enthusiast who children flock to. The musician with an amazing choir. The creative lead who fuels children's desire to paint. Find your thing and use it to fire children's enthusiasm for it.

6.   Help others. Many of the amazing heads I have spoken to developed their 'thing', then made a difference to those around them just by offering to help. It doesn't need to be a formal arrangement. Just find out what people need and offer assistance. Helping a colleague with some tricky data can enhance your skills further, develop those you help and establish you as a beginning leader. Notice what children (and their families) need, then – quietly – meet those needs. This also helps cement your place within the community. After all, parents aren't going to check out your CV to find out what you can do; they will watch to see what it is you actually do.

7.   Act as if you already have the role you aspire to. If you want others to see you as a leader or an expert in a particular area, behave like you are already. If you're passionate about a curriculum area and want to lead in that area, begin doing it. Demonstrate your impact with children and you are almost there. Share good practice and take on tasks or responsibilities as if you already have the role. Make

yourself the natural choice for a new role by already doing aspects of it.

8. Read widely and reflect deeply. You can add to your knowledge base and experience effectively by exposing yourself to new ideas, innovative ways of doing things, fresh systems and more. Questioning and reflecting on everything enables you to make sense of it, reject what's not relevant or won't work for you and embed what will work in your learning. Reflecting on your journey, the impact you have had with children (and the mistakes you have already made) helps you do more of the good stuff and avoid repeating patterns and behaviours that didn't help.

9. Know that you're good enough. Yes, you with the tiny voice! You're OK! There are no rules that you have to be a certain age or background for a particular role. Have confidence in your own abilities. Understand that if you think you can, there's a good chance you can. Realise that you may never feel 100% prepared, and ready enough is good enough for now. No one stepping into headship ever feels totally prepared anyway, no matter how confident they appear.

10. Look after yourself and surround yourself with the right people. Succeeding in education is a long game. You need to be able to keep going and that means a focus on self-care. There are times to push on and get important things done. There are times when we are all tired and we need to ease back a bit. That's natural. Want to be thought of as a ruthless leader? Be ruthless in looking after your own well-being.

All of us, whatever the stage of our educational journey, can learn from the wisdom of others. And all of us are worthy enough to add our voice to this collective wisdom. So, go on then – what are you going to say?

Oliver Wright is the sector manager for senior leadership at Twinkl. He has over 20 years' teaching experience, including 8 years as a head teacher. He has worked in a range of primary schools – from small, remote, rural settings to large, challenging city schools.

Part VI

Tiny Voices Talk About Ways to Find Your Voice

Over the course of my career, there have been times when I have 'lost' my voice and been unable to say what I think. Has this ever happened to you?

Have you ever sat in a meeting thinking that something just makes no sense, and yet you just smile and nod?

Have you ever received negative feedback because the person feeding back has not understood what you were doing? Were you able to clarify your aims or did you keep quiet for fear of making things worse?

Have you ever been talked over and decided that there is no point in saying anything as no one really cares about your opinion anyway?

I could go on, but there are so many reasons why we can lose our own voice or be reticent to use it.

I found that I lost my voice entirely when I entered the educational world online. I was terrified of posting something that someone might judge, so I didn't post anything. It was out of this fear of judgement that #TinyVoiceTalks on Twitter came about. I wanted to create somewhere where educators could find their voice without fear of incrimination. The podcast was built on the same premise and so was this book.

Over the years I have tended to keep quiet because I have feared judgement – possibly one of the reasons I remain beige – but keeping quiet is not always a good thing. We are continually encouraging the young people in our classrooms to find their voices, and yet we are often quite happy to muffle ours. Finding our voice is hard, especially if we have kept quiet for years.

There will always be those around you that have stronger opinions and louder voices, but that doesn't mean that you can't speak up. The following chapters will hopefully give you the ways and means to find your voice and recognise why finding it and using it is so important.

You owe it to yourself and the young people in your care to find your voice and have it heard. When tiny voices speak up, great things often happen!

Chapter 33

Big Wins for Tiny Voices

Amy Pickard

You, like me, might have a tiny voice. However, during my 20 years of teaching, I've noticed there are certain times when you just have to use that voice and, when you do, you win big.

Asking for help

Seeking assistance is most definitely not a sign of weakness. Sometimes we worry people will think we can't do our job if we ask for help, but it's actually quite the opposite. I have found asking for help to be an important part of my teacher's survival toolkit over the years. You might need support with something simple, or it may be a bigger challenge such as a behaviour issue. It's all OK. Always be prepared to say what you have tried already and be open to other suggestions when offered. Schools will have such a wealth of experience and ideas available to you, but if you don't ask for help, you don't discover new things. All staff at all levels have helped me on my journey.

Complimenting others

Everyone benefits from a compliment at any age! If you see something good, say so. Don't wait for what feels like the 'perfect occasion' as that often never arrives and then the moment will have passed. Watching that smile appear as you say something complimentary is just magical, and you are also helping to create a culture where compliments come your way too.

Checking in with others

If someone doesn't look themselves, ask them if they're OK. Then ask them again. Repeating this simple question can really ensure people get the support that they really need. This works, again, for any age.

When there's a problem

I've never liked confrontation, but I've discovered that identifying a problem does not necessarily lead to a showdown. In fact, directly raising an issue can actually diffuse a situation. This could be when a colleague's working style is very different to yours. Thinking of what the solution would be for you and raising it from this angle means you're not simply presenting the problem in a confrontational way. For example, you may ask to work out who is planning what subjects over the next term, so you have some advance warning if you don't like working in a last-minute way.

When you are worried about a child's progress

I've always worried about upsetting parents, especially when progress (or lack thereof) indicates there may be a special educational need issue to look into. Rather than beating delicately about the bush, I have discovered that being direct is actually well received by many parents. Often, they have been worrying too and I've had parents tell me they are so relieved when I have this conversation with them. The key is to ensure that you're not just telling a parent there is a problem, but you are explicit about the help you are going to give.

When getting the respect you deserve

Always remember that if anyone – child or adult – talks to you in a way that makes you feel uncomfortable, speak up! You have the right to be spoken to with respect, so never be afraid to let someone know if you find the way they are addressing you is unacceptable. It took me years to learn that when you ensure you are having a mutually respectful conversation, it really does help get things back on track.

Saying no!

I have to admit, responding in the negative is a work in progress for me. I've yet to train my mouth to do what my brain is telling it – just say no! Until I perfect this skill, I have found that replying to a request with 'Can I get back to you?' at least buys me some time to think.

It's not what you say but how you say it

Thinking before you speak and making little changes to how you would usually say things can make a huge difference. Rather than asking, 'What are you doing?', try, 'Are you OK?' Rather than demanding, 'Why are you late?', say, 'It's nice to see you today' (without teacher sarcasm!). Rather than insisting, 'You can't, until …', try 'You can, when …'.

*

So, go ahead, be brave and see the big wins you can have when you use that tiny voice of yours.

Amy Pickard is a primary school teacher who has been at the heart of education for 20 years. She has taught across the age range and led a wide range of subjects.

Chapter 34

When Tiny Voices Speak, You Listen

Fabian Darku

I was making my way in what you may call a 'fast-paced retail environment', but there was always that tiny voice, even then, nagging away at me, poking me ferociously to begin a search for fulfilment in an alternative direction. I knew I wanted to be the sort of person to make a difference to the attitudes and learning potential of young people. My tiny voice was telling me that I needed to be a teacher.

Looking back now over the start to my teaching career, I realised early on that my formula for professional satisfaction had two parts – I innately cared about the learners and also cared just as much about the teaching profession too. With these two powerful pillars in place, I knew that great things could be achieved.

From the outset of my career, I became an admirer of 'reflective practice', something that 'supports the development and maintenance of profession-al expertise'.[1] Looking back at what we did from the safety of the present allows us to rate and review our teaching practice, always with a view to continual improvement. Critical self-reflection can serve to quickly im-prove our practice ('Next time I'll try this instead') as well as support our longer-term development ('to improve I need to learn more about …'). In

---

1   Andrew Pollard, *Reflective Teaching in Schools*, 2nd edn (London: Bloomsbury, 2005), p. 5.

this way it can help build confidence too, helping us to see how and where we can always get better.

To help colleagues develop their own self-reflection skills, I developed what I call the RATE model:

1. Reflect – think about what happened in the lesson or over the course of the day/week/term.

2. Achievements – acknowledge what went well.

3. Targets – what specifically will you do to make future lessons even better?

4. Enforce – when will you make sure you have this done by?

This four-stage model is an enduring aspect of my own teaching practice and I continually use it to internally process the outcomes of my lessons, both formally when time allows or informally as often as I can.

Of course, no chapter reflecting on what we can do as professionals to raise our game would be complete without referring to the pressure we are under with marking, assessments and paperwork. Despite my love for the job and the way in which I knew I was making that difference to young people in my classes, I remember quickly becoming aware that I was drowning. It was a distressing feeling and the workload was detrimentally affecting my personal health too. Rather than blearily marking into the early hours each night, would that time have been better spent constructing ways to improve the educational experience for the learners? Should there be an increased focus, as a profession, on aspects such as our mental health as well as seeking alternative and engaging ways to implement innovative lesson content?

I was tired, irritable and constantly confused with the cracks I saw in the culture of an education system that allowed this imbalanced workload to become normal. What's more, I was becoming increasingly aware that I was losing sight of my own career goals, hidden as they were behind the unrelenting pressure to ensure the students met their attainment targets.

My tiny voice started speaking up again. There had to be another way.

I immersed myself in people and ideas that would feed my brain as I worked to improve things, for my students and for myself, from some of the best motivational speakers around, transformational researchers and educators like Carole Dweck and her work around growth mindsets. However, inspiration ended up coming from an unlikely source.

One evening, giving myself a rare break from marking, I found myself watching a programme called *Premier League Legends*. In this particular episode, they focused on ex-England international footballer Sol Campbell, who was explaining his controversial 2001 transfer from Tottenham Hotspur to bitter North London rival, Arsenal. What drove him was his sense of injustice at being on the periphery at Spurs, watching other players lift major trophies year after year, when he felt he had the ability and drive to accomplish such feats himself. In his words, he was desperate to 'be that scene' rather than be a spectator to the success of others.[2] In other words, he listened to his own tiny voice and made a momentous decision to switch allegiances – the right decision too, based on the trophies he went on to win with his new club.

If Sol's tiny voice could help him, what advice was my tiny voice offering me? The answer lay in blogging, and I suddenly realised that my voice could be put to good use helping other teachers facing similar challenges and dilemmas to my own. An early success for me in this new field was a blog entitled '5 tips to conquer a "mountain" of marking!', in which I suggested the following useful strategies:

1. Inform learners of the date their work will be returned to them.

2. Create a non-contact-time marking timetable (marking is completed at work in non-teaching periods).

3. Design an out-of-hours marking timetable.

4. Prioritise which work you mark and when (based on when you see your groups).

5. Collaborate with a colleague.[3]

---

2   *Premier League Legends*, Episode 2, 'Sol Campbell' [TV series] (Sky Sports, 2014).
3   Fabian A. Darku, 5 tips for teachers to conquer a 'mountain' of marking!, *FE Jobs* [blog](17 August 2018). Available at: https://www.fejobs.com/blog/5-tips-for-teachers-to-conquer-a-mountain-of-marking.

The recognition this blog received showed me that Sol Campbell was right. Tiny voices can help you with massive decisions when you listen and are then brave enough to act. I think of this as the Four Cs of the tiny voice crowd, if you like:

- *Confidence* – the best way to be confident is to act confidently. Every confident person is quaking inside. They just adapt and control that fear for themselves and hide it from you. Knowing your purpose and then sticking to it helps.

- *Creativity* – you will be amazed at the way in which confidence lets the creativity flow. With a clear vision and a sense of 'I don't know how I will do it, but I know that I will do it', ideas can really flourish.

- *Courage* – what's the worst that can happen and can you deal with that? We are far more resilient than we give ourselves credit for (think about the COVID-19 pandemic) so let that tiny voice become a roar!

- *Communication* – get that self-doubting, negative voice out of your head and onto Twitter, the blogosphere, the airwaves, the TeachMeets; wherever it may be that you will find interesting and generous professionals who love to hear from someone with something to say.

This tiny voice is now 40,000 words into a book of his own as well as grabbing the opportunity to speak on other platforms whenever possible. It would have been easy to have ended up bitter and twisted (and ill), marking books into the early hours, but I think God gives us tiny voices for a reason. It is down to us to listen to them and then be brave enough to follow their advice. And when other tiny voices hear ours, they too speak out.

Fabian Darku is a fully qualified teacher, teacher trainer, and teaching and learning leader working in secondary and further education since 2008.

Chapter 35

The First Rule of Book Club

Dave Tushingham

Like you, I love a good book about education. As we work to be more evidence informed as well as breaking new ground with our professional practice, books are the fuel for our creative flames. They can inform and inspire in equal measure, are a great starting point for reflecting on what to do and are equally a great setting-off point for breaking all the rules and trying something no one has ever done before.

The trouble is there are more books than there is time; how do we know which are the best ones to be investing some of that special time in? This is where the school book club comes in – making sure some of the world's best thinking about education can be accessed by more staff more easily. An effective book club is an attempt to create a safe place for staff to learn and to share, and for great practice to grow organically across the school.

I was fortunate enough to be there at the birth of my secondary school's book club, inspired by our head of department, so let me share with you some points to consider and lessons we learned to help you in creating your own book club.

What do you want your book club to achieve?

- Know your staff, school, students and community well. How does the book club fit into your school improvement plan, for example?

- Where are the identified areas of need? What do you want the 'golden thread' to be? Teaching and learning? Behaviour? Creative curriculum design? Inclusion? Something else? How will you ensure unbiased diversity and richness of the texts shared (and not just the books cashing in on the latest fad)?

- Will your book club be used for instructional or non-instructional coaching?

- Is it designed to be a tool for leaders and mentors in your academy to use for their bespoke needs, or will it be more general, allowing teachers to go where their interests lie?

- How scripted do you want the sessions to be?

- How will you measure its impact? How will you know that it has supported classroom practice, if that is its purpose?

- What are its limitations? What are the similarities and differences you expect to see in each session? What is the book club *not*?

Communication is key

- What does your 'brand' look like? Do you record your sessions? Who are the best-placed members of staff to organise and host the sessions? How long should each session be? How regularly should they be held? Should they be virtual, in person or mixed? Will consistency in the use of logos, jingles and scripts breed familiarity or make it seem a bit too corporate?

- Keep communication succinct. Share the reading material beforehand.

- Will the invitation be open or selective? If the latter, how many people will you invite, how will you invite them and how can you – or should you even try to – make sure they attend? How will you interact with staff who engage after the session? What incentives might you offer (biscuits and bookmarks go down well!)?

- Have a clear structure for sharing the session notes afterwards and what you expect staff to do – if anything – as a result of the session.

Small and regular

- Share small extracts that complement the identified focus with any intended future actions.

- Keep scripts granular and easy to digest.

- Keep any takeaways to a single action step that can be taken into the classroom for implementation and reflection.

- Ensure that the 'golden thread' through the sessions gives the opportunity for staff to revisit their new knowledge and reflect on their practice. Did it help? Did it make things worse?

Aim high

- Don't assume prior knowledge, but do have high levels of challenge in the pedagogical material that is discussed.

- Make sure the sessions are low stakes. Colleagues come to grow, not feel small.

- Do you record the sessions so that the resource can go on to reach a wider audience and, if so, who and how?

- Are there senior members of staff or others such as the author who can add expertise to the discussion?

Our club was designed to run twice per term. The first session would be a pedagogical extract and the second would be more specific to our particular team – in my case, maths. This allowed us to pursue a deeper understanding of how the pedagogical ideas fitted into the subject-specific context. We would send out a book extract a week before the session with prompt questions to support our reading, and we would record and consider any reflections that came to us. It wouldn't matter if we didn't have any. The sessions were chaired by our head of department and my role was to share my reflections on the text and why this book – and this particular extract – had been chosen. Sometimes we were lucky enough to have the author join us to talk about their own reflections on their writing. Other participants would then join the discussion, with the author involved as a participant too. I would also participate, asking provocative questions or ones designed to direct the conversation towards key points from the extract (or sometimes just to help my own practice).

Discussion and questions had a natural flow and it was always fine if some preferred to participate by simply listening. The discussions would culminate in us all choosing one takeaway which we would record and make into a sketch note. This, along with a video and podcast, then helped us share the event with a wider audience.

Our book club is designed to be a resource that can be dipped in and out of. It is available for senior leaders and mentors as a resource for supporting new and inexperienced members of staff, as well as our more passive or perhaps reluctant colleagues. It may be a 'required listening' element of whole-staff continuing professional development (CPD) as determined by the senior leadership team (SLT) or selected by individual staff who may be offering a CPD programme to a department, staff body or a wider audience. Anyone is welcome to participate – we have had SLT members attend to support the development of part of the school improvement plan, and trainee teachers yet to embark on their initial teacher training picking out their own takeaways ready for their first classroom experience. The resources are also all free to use on the school website.

Although your book club might not involve multimedia recordings or guest appearances, it still has the potential to offer excellent development opportunities for you and your colleagues, acting as a model of great teaching and learning across the school. Do it well and you will have soon mastered the first rule of book club – everyone talks about book club.

Dave Tushingham is a lead practitioner in a school in Bristol and can be followed on Twitter: @davetushingham. Dave is a current fellow with the Chartered College of Teaching and a professional development lead for the National Centre of Excellence in the Teaching of Mathematics, following his passion for continued professional development. Dave is co-founder of the #GLTBookClub alongside Rhiannon Rainbow, the school improvement lead for mathematics for the Greenshaw Learning Trust.

Chapter 36

Finding Your Voice Through a Subject Association

Dr Brendan O'Sullivan

As recently as the early 2000s in Ireland, calculators were not used until students had finished their Junior Certificate, at the age of about 15. When the possibility of younger children being allowed to use them in their maths lessons was brought up, controversy raged. Some experts were of the view that calculators would do irreparable damage to numeracy. Others argued that their introduction would, in fact, help students, enabling them to focus on the maths rather than struggling with the arithmetic. What were we teachers to do?

A teacher's early career is bolstered by lots of support when faced with difficult questions. Before we enter the classroom, university lecturers and tutors instruct us on what it means to be a teacher and expose us to the modern methodologies of the time. Once newly qualified, colleagues act as mentors and help us to meet the needs of the students and the schools in which we teach. However, what happens when there's a question that goes beyond the expertise of the immediate school staff, like the great calculator question?[1]

---

1   Calculators were introduced from June 2003.

Change is an ongoing feature of education. Having moved on from being a newly qualified teacher, it is easy for the recently qualified to quickly feel like an imposter. What's more, as time passes, all experienced teachers will have different queries in relation to the teaching of their subject. To combat this, it is vital for teachers to extend their network far and wide in order to access the latest and best information. I believe that their subject association can go a long way to assisting teachers at this point and, indeed, for the rest of their career.

In more recent times, we all wondered about the best way to help our students through the use of technology when faced with home learning during the COVID-19 pandemic. While this way of working was new to many (perhaps most) teachers, it was not itself a new phenomenon and had been present for decades. Through the many subject associations, expert advice was made available to support colleagues with school routines such as taking a roll call online, presenting work virtually, electronically setting and sending out assignments, and returning marked material to students. Teachers across the country were quick to harness the power of blended learning platforms to continue the teaching and learning for their students, thanks to subject associations' experts coming to the fore.

Such support is something that has happened in the past, allayed the fears of teachers during the recent pandemic and, I have no doubt, will continue into the future.

Teachers – and not only those just starting out – can be reluctant to speak in a forum of their peers. They can often feel that they don't have anything of value to contribute and might be self-conscious in such a group. Thankfully, the subject associations are aware of this and especially value and encourage the contribution of such tiny voices. They are quick to make new entrants to the profession feel at home and allow them genuine opportunities to express their views and share their opinions. By facilitating the voice of teachers in this way, the subject association enables teachers to feel valued and can assure them that their concerns, so often for their students, are actually shared by many.

All these associations share a common aim – to further the study and teaching of their given subject. This is facilitated by fostering cooperation between teachers at all levels. As a post-primary maths specialist, I have benefitted from input from primary school teachers as well as from university professors. From how students engaged with maths before they came to my classroom to what they will need to know if and when they go on into further education, each contribution offered me a different perspective on my practice.

The list of activities conducted by subject associations is practically endless. For example, they offer lectures, debates and symposia, in the virtual as well as the real world, to inform teachers and keep them in touch with the burning issues of the profession. They also allow teachers to voice their concerns and receive important advice and support. Another of their vital services involves maintaining a constant review of curricula and examination papers. New content can be introduced into any reformed curricula and teachers can sometimes be left confused by the professional development that is provided by state bodies. The subject association, knowing the demands of their subject best, can put together a programme that will serve to bring teachers quickly and accurately up to speed with any new requirements.

Similarly, a subject association can act as a watchdog when it comes to examinations and examination boards, pointing out aspects of assessment that are unfair or could undermine the efforts of students to demonstrate what they know. Every June, teachers across Ireland meet to discuss the recent examinations and submit reports that are sent to the chief examiners of each subject.[2] These reports are taken on board when the marking schemes are being formulated. Indeed, a subject association offers many professional benefits, and I have only scratched the surface here.

If I were to offer one piece of advice to any teacher, especially one with a tiny voice, it would be to join your subject association. You will be amazed how it can benefit and support your practice, which in turn will benefit your students and their learning.

Dr Brendan O'Sullivan has been a post-primary teacher for over 20 years and is currently teaching mathematics at Davis College, Mallow, Co. Cork. He holds master's degrees in education and mathematics and completed his doctorate degree in 2017. He acts as a subject advisor to the Irish Teaching Council and has served as a mentor to newly qualified teachers as part of the National Induction Programme for Teachers.

---

2   In Ireland one centralised body (the State Examinations Commission) sets the exams, unlike in other places where there are various examination boards.

Chapter 37
You Be You

Toria Husband

So much of the great practice I have learned in nearly 20 years of teaching is the result of my good fortune. I am lucky enough to have been mentored and coached by truly some of the best leaders that our education system is privileged to have. I have learned from the best. The thing is, I have learned from the worst too: I have been lucky enough, although it might not have felt it at the time, to have looked around me and learned what *not* to do. I am using my tiny voice to share both sides.

Finding your voice

Even if you are new to teaching, you can and should speak up. For example, never let anyone make you feel that you don't have anything useful to add to staff meetings until you have a certain number of years of classroom practice under your belt. No one will ever be able to define how many years that is anyway, and if the merit of anyone's contribution is down to the years on the job, there will always be someone more experienced than you to say your opinion isn't valid.

Your opinion is *always* valid, no matter how long you have been at the chalkface (or SmartBoardface or Zoomface). Yes, you may be suggesting an idea many of us have tried before which hasn't worked, but who knows? Maybe this time, in this context, it could. Maybe you're the one who can make it work – the missing piece of the jigsaw.

Even as an experienced teacher and leader, there will so often be someone who knows more than I do. And that's OK. Experience has taught me to find the middle ground, to consider the feelings of others before I rush in with an idea of how to change the world for the better, to ask for advice, to sound out an idea first. As a leader, the buck might stop with me, but I want to hear what my team has to say first – and that includes you.

The loudest voice is sometimes just the biggest ego

After so many years of my life spent listening to people in staff briefings, department meetings, senior leadership team (SLT) meetings and more, I have learned a simple fact – there will always be people who speak for the sake of speaking. They insist on being heard, but you realise that the more they speak, the less they have to say.

I have to admit, I was always in awe of these erudite professionals. I would walk away from meetings feeling like I had contributed so little. Then, reflecting on what had happened, I would realise that they had actually dominated the meeting, making it impossible for anyone to speak, making it all about them. This has been a common thread throughout my career.

I remember an interview for a Future Leaders programme, and again later for subsequent leadership roles, completing the inevitable 'goldfish bowl' element, the one where all the applicants work together on a set task, observed by the interview panel. My feedback always revolved around the fact that I wasn't vocal enough. What I know now is that those tasks really just demonstrate who has the biggest ego.

Even now, in a meeting, I will be the one taking notes, thinking, scribbling, making connections, working out solutions to the issues raised. Experience now makes me accept that this is no bad thing. I speak when I have something to say, and the best teams I have worked in understand and accept that. They value my voice because they know that I can be relied on to summarise debates and offer solutions, and because I have listened. They know that when I have something to say it will be well considered, and then they listen.

Great teamwork comes from recognising and valuing the individual roles people play in a team, and that starts with recognising the value everyone brings – including your own.

Don't be in a hurry to define yourself

You might be sitting there with your 10-year professional career plan all mapped out. If you have one, great. But I've been there, done that, ripped it up. The thing is, working life is not always quite so clear cut, and progress through your career is never a straight line. And that's a good thing.

Coming into teaching at the grand old age of 28 meant that I felt pressure to progress at speed and prove myself. Like many others, I felt the path was clearly defined – academic or pastoral routes were the choices, with either being a suitable route to senior leadership.

I put my ball firmly in the academic court and quickly had a teaching and learning responsibility post for personal, social and health education (PSHE) during my first year as a teacher (I later discovered the role to be the hot potato which no one wanted – I loved it though). Next step was head of department for my main subject, drama. So far so good, and all going to plan. Next stop, head of faculty. The problem was that the school then threw a curveball and decided not to keep the head of faculty role. That had been my intended stepping stone! How was I supposed to get to assistant head now?! My lovely straight-line trajectory had hit a brick wall.

I was now faced with a choice: stay at the school I loved, where I was valued and felt I made a difference, or move on and take a chance somewhere else. Even though it was not what I had originally planned, I opted to stay put. I was so pleased that I did. It's amazing how far you can get by going nowhere. In staying, I was able to develop as a teacher and a leader, and, more importantly, develop much deeper connections not just across the school but with the wider community too.

I was also fortunate enough to have the best head teachers as mentors and role models: one just prior to his retirement, then two subsequent co-head teachers. They believed in me, even when I didn't, and knew when I was ready for a greater challenge, supporting me through different leadership programmes. Their belief in me and my hard work paid off. I was appointed onto the SLT with responsibility for post-16 – something that was most definitely not part of the original plan.

I had never considered myself as a pastoral person, let alone a data person. This new role pushed me out of my comfort zone and really gave me the opportunity to experience it all. In hindsight, I should have let go of the role I still had as head of drama. My time was spread far too thinly as I was pulled in so many different directions; however, this was my first real opportunity to prove what I could do as a leader so, of course, I jumped right in.

Was I successful? I'd like to think so, at least in some respects. I was definitely a voice for the young people who didn't feel that they had one of their own. Did I make mistakes? Oh yes! But, most importantly, I've learned from them.

Then it was time to walk away because, well, life.

I've never been so upset to leave a job, but I knew the time was right. I remember my mum telling me when I was young that, one day, I'd realise that there was more to life than a job. How right she was. The plan (that word again) was to spend more time with her, but that took on a different meaning when she was diagnosed with terminal cancer. My previous decision to leave my job did mean, though, that I was there for her every step along the way: the joyful moments in adversity, the difficult ones at treatment and consultations, then all day and night at the hospice at the end. That is time that I will never have again and although I walked out on a job and a school I loved, it was absolutely the right thing to do. I'd do it again in a heartbeat. In fact, I wished I had done it sooner to give me more time to enjoy life to the full.[1]

It is now 5 years later, my 10-year plan is in shreds and I feel like I'm starting again; older but definitely wiser. I now feel lucky to have once again found a setting where my knowledge and experience are valued – somewhere I feel I can make a difference every day and with an outstanding head teacher who models all the values I believe in.

----

1   And here's another thing I have learned – it's difficult to be taken seriously once your CV takes a detour. I'm not a mother but, having taken time out, I can understand some of the problems returning mothers have in terms of progression. This needs to change.

Trust your instincts

Know when to walk – or even run – away. Some schools are toxic, but that's actually quite easy to spot if you know where to look. The big challenge is the ones that aren't toxic but just aren't the right fit for you. These can be much harder to work out in advance.

If you feel like you don't fit in, that lessons aren't going so well, that things just aren't going smoothly, you end up doubting yourself and your ability. Then you end up doubting your chosen vocation. I've seen so many good teachers walk away from the profession because they were simply in the wrong place. Before you take such a big step, always ask yourself first – is it worth trying a different school, a different phase, a completely different setting? After returning to teaching, I have to admit I went through such a period of doubt myself. There were no real issues, I just wasn't feeling it any more. The students were great, the staff were great and I was pretty much left to get on with things. I just wasn't enjoying it. Now what?

As ever, fate stepped in again. A local (Catholic) school needed help for a term before a new teacher started, and I volunteered. It was here I fell in love with teaching again. From the moment I walked through the doors, I knew this was a place where I would feel happy.

I was greeted by the head teacher and immediately felt like I belonged to this wonderful family she had created. There was warmth, compassion and a genuine interest taken in every single person. It was a community where everyone was respected and valued. Remember I said that it's easy to spot the toxic schools if you know where to look? It's easy to spot the truly wonderful schools too. For example, the school video here wasn't the traditional staged corporate promo, it was an honest 360° video of all students having fun on their Saint's Day, representing multiple faiths and communities. It genuinely captured the school and its environment. I knew it would be a place in which I felt privileged to work.

In all of the schools where I've been happiest, I've known I would be from the moment I stepped through the doors. In my very first school, before I was even a qualified teacher and was working as a learning mentor, I knew it the moment the assistant head teacher had stopped mid-tour to talk to a child who was waiting outside her office. If you go on a tour of a school during an interview, be wary of the places where you are carefully guided, the corporate speeches you are given and the answers you don't get to your questions.

I'm now at a point in my career where I can be selective about where I choose to apply and where I accept an interview. The right school will be out there for you.

Remember, too, that an interview is a two-way process. It's easy to forget that, especially when you are still searching for your first job and it seems like everyone else around you is sorted. Make sure you ask – and get answers to – all the questions you have. Think about your own development too and ask what the school can offer you. Make sure you visit too, if you can. The best schools I know have adapted well and tried very hard to make the experience as welcoming as possible to potential candidates.

Don't walk in anyone else's shoes (no matter how pretty)

Forge your own path and have faith in your own abilities and ideas. Most jobs in schools involve stepping into someone else's shoes: your new class may have had a favourite teacher before you showed up; you may be taking on the role of a previously successful leader and feel the pressure to be as good as they were; or you might be entering a tightly knit team who are opposed to change. Whatever the role and shoes to be filled, you are not that previous person and nor should you be. I've been down this road, beating myself up for not being my perfect predecessor. It's when you realise that you can never live up to them, and stop trying to, that you see things more clearly. This was a big wake-up call for me. Now I could spot things, like, for a start, they had double the time I had been given, so of course they were going to be able to do more!

Wearing my own shoes meant I learned to prioritise. I couldn't be all things to all people with the limited time I had, so I pinpointed the things I *could* do which would make a difference. I also realised I had different values and brought a different approach both to staff and students. I couldn't run staff meetings, assemblies and so on like they were run before because that just wasn't me. Once I figured that out, everything changed for the better.

Be compassionate

The best head teachers and leaders I have been lucky enough to work with have had compassion at the core of everything they do. I didn't always agree with them, but I know that every decision they took was always made with the best interest of the children, the staff and the community at the heart.

Sometimes it was the small things that made this compassion evident – the Post-it note left on your desk after an observation or the Wispa bar in your pigeonhole, just because. And then there were the bigger things like always knowing the head teacher's door was open to all staff and students, for any reason. Not to mention scooping me up (literally) off the floor when my mum had her first emergency hospital admission and packing me off to see her, after making sure I was safe to drive.

In times of crisis and community tragedy, that compassion from a leader is critical. The way they handle those events tells you everything you need to know about them as a person and as a leader.

The best leaders I've worked with have opened up the school to the community during floods, making sure everyone was fed and had somewhere safe to sleep. They've helped a community to grieve over the death of students and colleagues, even when they were grieving themselves.

Some leaders deal with things differently. Maybe they haven't taken the time to get to know the community or they effectively barricade their office doors so the school community doesn't know them. I know which type of leader I would always want to follow.

Someone once said to me that choosing a school is a bit like being on a ship. Do you trust your captain to steer you not only through the calm waters but also through the dangerous storm? Or would they be one of the first on the lifeboat? I always think of that when I visit a school.

You be you

I was told in the early days of my career that I wasn't aggressive or assertive enough to be a leader. Someone once described my approach as 'strategic with a heart'. I'll take that, thank you very much! You can be strong and still be kind. You can take those tough decisions and hold staff to account but still be caring at the same time.

One head teacher I worked with didn't wish the young people luck as he ended his leavers' assemblies. Instead, he finished with that quote from Cinderella: 'Have courage and be kind.' I always think this was also an accurate description of his leadership.

I've reached a point in life and my career now where I know the sort of teacher and leader I am but, more importantly, I know the person I am. I know what I value. That has given me clarity about what I want from a role, from a school, from a leader. I won't compromise on the things I believe about education or what all young people have a right to expect. I am (back) in a role which combines the things I love most – developing staff to become the best they can be, giving young people a chance to have a brighter future and helping them to find their voice. What more can we wish for from the amazing job of being a teacher?

A founding fellow of the Chartered College of Teaching, Toria Husband has led performing arts departments, personal, social and economic education and post-16, and has been on SLTs in large mainstream secondary schools. Toria is now about to embark on a new opportunity to lead on teaching and learning, and professional development, in a large pupil peferral unit in South Yorkshire.

Final Thoughts

Writing this, I feel overcome with emotion. Never in a million years, when I created a hashtag on Twitter, did I think that I would be lucky enough to be putting together a book that celebrates the tiny voices in education. When I was a little girl, I said that I wanted to publish a book by the time I was 30. I am 20 years late, but it took time and experience to realise how important my voice and that of others is. Our voices are truly gifts that we need to celebrate.

When I was at school, I often asked 'why'. I wanted to know why pi is 3.14 and why calaulating the percentage of water of crystallisation is worked out in the way it is. I was often told 'because it is', but to my mind that wasn't a sufficient answer. I was probably a complete pain in maths and science lessons because I asked 'why' all the time. That is until I learned to stop asking. I would look at others in the class who would shake their heads when I would ask 'why'. They were happy just to accept without needing further explanation, and I realised that I was just an annoying noise in the corner. So I began to keep quiet.

It has always been my uniqueness that has worried me. I am incredibly enthusiastic, passionate and a bit like a dog with a bone. Some people don't like that, finding it incredibly grating, but I have a choice – I can keep quiet as I did in school, or I can be me and speak out. I know now that, to a degree, we are all like Marmite and no one is going to get on with everyone. Some of us are more 'Marmitey' than others, but that's OK – we just need to surround ourselves with those people who truly hear us, support us and believe in us. Sometimes they will be close at hand, but we often have to look for them.

Why is finding our voice important? Because in our schools and class-rooms we are teaching our future. Yes, those young people in front of you each day are our future teachers, politicians, athletes, authors, doctors, scientists and so much more. They need role models who are not afraid to use their voice but, more than that, they need educators who are willing to speak up and do the right thing by them. That sometimes means we have to challenge what we are being told to do, or at the very least ask questions.

So, look for opportunities to use your voice and share your thoughts. This could be in the staff room, staff meetings or chats with colleagues. It might be by attending educational events and chatting to like-minded educators, or you might consider starting a blog. Blogging is a wonderful way to find your voice and express your opinions – if you are worried about being judged, write it anonymously. I find writing cathartic and a way of ex-pressing what I think from the comfort of my house. Finding my voice in this way often helps me to clarify my thoughts and ideas around a subject which gives me the courage to air them to others at a later date.

Go on podcasts (not that I am plugging *Tiny Voice Talks* at all) and once you have found your voice enough, speak at events. By finding your voice, you can empower others to find theirs.

Your voice matters and so do you.

Now spread your wings and fly!

Space for Your Voice

When the whole world is silent, even one voice becomes powerful.

Malala Yousafzai[1]

Please use the next few pages to capture your own thoughts.

---

1   Malala Yousafzai, *I am Malala* (London: Weidenfeld & Nicolson, 2014).

References

Anna Freud NCCF, Childhood trauma and the brain | UK Trauma Council [video], *YouTube* (27 September 2020). Available at: https://www.youtube.com/watch?v=xY-BUY1kZpf8&t=10s.

Bomber, Louise (2007). *Inside I'm Hurting: Practical Strategies for Supporting Children with Attachment Difficulties in Schools*. London: Worth Publishing.

Bridge, Jeffrey A., Horowitz, Lisa M., Fontanella, Cynthia A., Sheftall, Arielle H., Greenhouse, Joel, Kelleher, Kelly J. and Campo, John V. (2018). Age-related racial disparity in suicide rates among US youths from 2001 through 2015, *JAMA Pediatrics* 172(7): 697–699.

Brooks, Maegan P. and Houck, Davis W. (eds) (2011). *The Speeches of Fannie Lou Hamer: To Tell It Like It Is*. Jackson, MS: University Press of Mississippi.

Brown, Brené (2010). *The Gifts of Imperfection: Let Go of Who You Think You're Supposed to Be and Embrace Who You Are*. Center City, MN: Hazelden Publishing.

Brown, Brené (2010). The power of vulnerability [video], *TED* (June). Available at: https://www.ted.com/talks/brene_brown_the_power_of_vulnerability?language=en.

Centre for Mental Health (2022). Fact sheet: children and young people's mental health (27 April). Available at: https://www.centreformentalhealth.org.uk/fact-sheet-children-and-young-peoples-mental-health.

Clark, Richard (1989). When teaching kills learning. Cited in Becton Loveless (2022), A complete guide to schema theory and its role in education, *Education Corner* (12 April). Available at: https://www.educationcorner.com/schema-theory/.

Connor, Mary and Pokora, Julia (2017). *Coaching and Mentoring at Work: Developing Effective Practice*, 3rd edn. London: Open University Press.

Covey, Stephen R. (1989). *The 7 Habits of Highly Effective People*. New York: Simon & Schuster.

Csikszentmihalyi, Mihaly (1990). *Flow: The Psychology of Optimal Experience*. New York: Harper and Row.

Csikszentmihalyi, Mihaly (1998). *Finding Flow: The Psychology of Engagement with Everyday Life*. New York: Basic Books.

Czarnec, Jeffrey and Hill, Michelle G. (2018). Schemata and Instructional Strategies, *The EvoLLLution*. Available at: https://evolllution.com/programming/teaching-and-learning/schemata-and-instructional-strategies/.

Darku, Fabian A. (2018). 5 tips for teachers to conquer a 'mountain' of marking! *FE Jobs* [blog] (17 August). Available at: https://www.fejobs.com/blog/5-tips-for-teachers-to-conquer-a-mountain-of-marking.

Department for Education (2014). *The Equality Act 2010 and Schools: Departmental Advice for School Leaders, School Staff, Governing Bodies and Local Authorities* (May). Available at: https://assets.publishing.service.gov.uk/government/uploads/system/uploads/attachment_data/file/315587/Equality_Act_Advice_Final.pdf.

Department of Health and Social Care (2019). *UK Chief Medical Officers' Physical Activity Guidelines*. Available at: https://assets.publishing.service.gov.uk/government/uploads/

system/uploads/attachment_data/file/832868/uk-chief-medical-officers-physical-activity-guidelines.pdf.

Devine, Mary, Meyers, Raymond and Houssemand, Claude (2013). How can coaching make a positive impact within educational settings? *Procedia-Social and Behavioral Sciences* 93: 1382–1389.

Dreyfus, Hubert L. and Dreyfus, Stuart E. (1986). *Mind over Machine: The Power of Human Intuition and Expertise in the Age of the Computer.* New York: Free Press.

Education Support Partnership (2018). *Teacher Wellbeing Index 2018.* Available at: http://downloads2.dodsmonitoring.com/downloads/Misc_Files/teacher_wellbeing_index_2018.pdf.

Eliot, George (1872). *Middlemarch.* Edinburgh: William Blackwood and Sons.

EY (2019). *The Value of Dyslexia: Dyslexic Capability and Organisations of the Future.* Available at: https://assets.ey.com/content/dam/ey-sites/ey-com/en_uk/topics/diversity/ey-the-value-of-dyslexia-dyslexic-capability-and-organisations-of-the-future.pdf.

Ferfolja, Tania and Stavrou, Efty (2015). Workplace experiences of Australian lesbian and gay teachers: findings from a national survey, *Canadian Journal of Educational Administration and Policy* 173: 113–138. Available at: https://files.eric.ed.gov/fulltext/EJ1083427.pdf.

F4Demo, The biology of toxic stress [video], *YouTube* (22 December 2017). Available at: https://www.youtube.com/watch?v=Z4CD6jyWw2A&t=5s.

Garvey, Robert, Megginson, David and Stokes, Paul (2010). *Coaching and Mentoring: Theory and Practice.* London: Sage.

Grant, Anthony M., Green, Suzy and Rynsaardt, Josephine (2010). Developmental coaching for high school teachers: executive coaching goes to school, *Consulting Psychology Journal: Practice and Research* 62(3): 151–168.

Hanson, Jamie L. and Nacewicz, Brendon M. (2021). Amygdala allostasis and early life adversity: considering excitotoxicity and inescapability in the sequelae of stress, *Frontiers in Human Neuroscience* 15: 624705. DOI. 10.3389/fnhum.2021.624705.

Hargreaves, Eleanore and Rolls, Luke (2021). *Unlocking Research: Reimagining Professional Development in Schools.* Abingdon: Routledge.

Hill, Maisie (2019). *Period Power: Harness Your Hormones and Get Your Cycle Working for You.* London: Green Tree Publishing.

Hughes, Haili (2021). *Mentoring in Schools: How to Become an Expert Colleague – Aligned with the Early Career Framework.* Carmarthen: Crown House Publishing.

Ibarra, Herminia (2015). *Act Like a Leader, Think Like a Leader.* Boston, MA: Harvard Business Review Press.

Klass, Perri (2020). The benefits of exercise for children's mental health, *New York Times* (2 March). Available at: https://www.nytimes.com/2020/03/02/well/family/the-benefits-of-exercise-for-childrens-mental-health.html.

Kline, Nancy (2020). *The Promise That Changes Everything: I Won't Interrupt You.* London: Penguin Random House.

Kohn, Alfie (2018). *Punished by Rewards,* 25th anniversary edn. London: Mariner Books.

Mandolesi, Laura, Polverino, Arianna, Montuori, Simone, Foti, Francesca, Ferraioli, Giampaolo, Sorrentino, Pierpaolo and Sorrentino, Giuseppe (2018). Effects of physical exercise on cognitive functioning and wellbeing: biological and psychological benefits, *Frontiers in Psychology* 9: 509. DOI. 10.3389/fpsyg.2018.00509.

McFall, Matthew (2018). *The Little Book of Awe and Wonder: A Cabinet of Curiosities*. Carmarthen: Independent Thinking Press.

Medina, John (2008). Schema [video], *YouTube*. Available at: https://www.youtube.com/watch?v=mzbRpMlEHzM.

Mehren, Aylin, Özyurt, Jale, Lam, Alexandra P., Brandes, Mirko, Müller, Helge H. O., Thiel, Christiane M. and Philipsen, Alexandra (2019). Acute effects of aerobic exercise on executive function and attention in adult patients with ADHD, *Frontiers in Psychiatry* 10: 132. DOI. 10.3389/fpsyt.2019.00132.

Michalak, Katja (2019). Schema (cognitive), *Encyclopædia Britannica*. Available at: https://www.britannica.com/science/schema-cognitive.

Mulvenney, Sheila (2020). Reflections on regulation, *Attuned Education* [blog] (30 July). Available at: https://attunededucation.com/2020/07/30/reflections-on-regulation/.

MindShift (2015). Ken Robinson: Creativity is in everything, especially teaching, *KQED* (22 April). Available at: https://www.kqed.org/mindshift/40217/sir-ken-robinson-creativity-is-in-everything-especially-teaching.

Myatt, Mary (2018). *The Curriculum: Gallimaufry to Coherence*. Woodbridge: John Catt Educational.

National College for School Leadership (2005). *Leading Coaching in Schools*. London: NCSL.

Pennsylvania Department of Education (2021). Activating student schema. Available at: http://pdcenter.pdesas.org/CourseRendering/CourseContent/Render/2360701951680272481880031140510351602131632377114.

Pierson, Rita (2013). Every kid needs a champion [video], *TED* (May). Available at: https://www.ted.com/talks/rita_pierson_every_kid_needs_a_champion?language=en.

Pollard, Andrew (2005). *Reflective Teaching in Schools*, 2nd edn. London: Bloomsbury.

Richman-Abdou, Kelly (2022). Kintsugi: the centuries-old art of repairing broken pottery with gold, *My Modern Met* (5 March). Available at: https://mymodernmet.com/kintsugi-kintsukuroi/.

Robertson, Juliet (2014). *Dirty Teaching: A Beginner's Guide to Learning Outdoors*. Carmarthen: Independent Thinking Press.

Rosenshine, Barak (2012). Principles of instruction: research-based strategies that all teachers should know, *American Educator* 36(1): 12–19.

Rundell, Katherine (2017). *The Explorer*. London: Bloomsbury.

Schnall, Marianne (2010). Exclusive interview with Dr Jane Goodall, *HuffPost* (1 June). Available at: https://www.huffpost.com/entry/exclusive-interview-with_b_479894.

Supovitz, Jonathan, Sirinides, Philip and May, Henry (2010). How principals and peers influence teaching and learning, *Educational Administration Quarterly* 46(1): 31–56.

University of Exeter (2021). One in six children has probable mental disorder in 2021 – continuing 2020 peak, (30 September). Available at: https://www.exeter.ac.uk/news/research/title_879721_en.html.

US Department of Health and Human Services (2018). *Physical Activity Guidelines for Americans*, 2nd edn. Available at: https://health.gov/sites/default/files/2019-09/Physical_Activity_Guidelines_2nd_edition.pdf.

Van Nieuwerburgh, Christian (2020). *An Introduction to Coaching Skills: A Practical Guide*. Thousand Oaks, CA: Sage.

Weaver, Matthew (2016). Marketing firm posts 'only dyslexics need apply' job advert, *The Guardian* (11 February). Available at: https://www.theguardian.com/society/2016/feb/11/job-advertisement-uk-thinktank-recruit-dyslexics-only-steve-jobs-garage.

Western, Simon (2012). *Coaching and Mentoring: A Critical Text*. Thousand Oaks, CA: Sage.

Willingham, Daniel (2010). *Why Don't Students Like School?* San Francisco, CA: Jossey-Bass.

Yousafzai, Malala (2014). *I am Malala*. London: Weidenfeld & Nicolson.

About the author

Toria is a primary teacher who has worked in many roles in the primary sector for more than 20 years. She is also a coach and is committed to empowering the voices around her – both of the large and small kind. Her love of teaching means that she is always keen to learn from others and hone her craft. In February 2020, she created the #TinyVoiceTalks community on Twitter and later that year she created the *Tiny Voice Talks* podcast. Since these started, she has managed to raise the voices of many educators and share good practice far and wide. In 2021, Toria was the recipient of a Rising Star Award in the educational field. Toria became a fellow of the Chartered College of Teaching in 2020.

Tiny Voice Talks is an award-winning podcast that gives a platform to the quieter voices in education. In it, Toria chats to teachers, leaders, authors and advisors about what they are doing and how this is impacting on the young people in our classrooms.

If you are in education and want your voice heard, contact Toria on tinyvoicetalks@gmail.com.

To join #TinyVoiceTalks on Twitter just find Toria's pinned tweet each Tuesday (@toriaclaire).

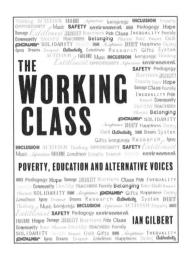

The Working Class
Poverty, education and alternative voices

Edited by Ian Gilbert

ISBN: 978-178135278-6

In *The Working Class*, Ian Gilbert unites educators from across the UK and further afield to call on all those working in schools to adopt a more enlightened and empathetic approach to supporting children in challenging circumstances.

One of the most intractable problems in modern education is how to close the widening gap in attainment between the haves and the have-nots. Unfortunately, successive governments both in the UK and abroad have gone about solving it the wrong way.

Independent Thinking founder Ian Gilbert's increasing frustration with educational policies that favour 'no excuses' and 'compliance', and that ignore the broader issues of poverty and inequality, is shared by many others across the sphere of education – and this widespread disaffection has led to the assembly of a diverse cast of teachers, school leaders, academics and poets who unite in this book to challenge the status quo. Their thought-provoking commentary, ideas and impassioned anecdotal insights are presented in the form of essays, think pieces and poems that draw together a wealth of research on the issue and probe and discredit the current view on what is best for children from poorer socio-economic backgrounds. Exploring themes such as inclusion, aspiration, pedagogy and opportunity, the contributions collectively lift the veil of feigned 'equality of opportunity for all' to reveal the bigger picture of poverty and to articulate the hidden truth that there is always another way.

Written for policy makers and activists as well as school leaders and educators, *The Working Class* is both a timely survey of the impact of current policies and an invaluable source of practical advice on what can be done to better support disadvantaged children in the school system.

www.crownhouse.co.uk

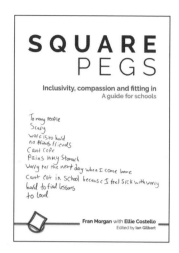

Square Pegs

Inclusivity, compassion and fitting in – a guide for schools

Fran Morgan, with Ellie Costello
Edited by Ian Gilbert

ISBN: 978-178135410-0

A book for educators who find themselves torn between a government/Ofsted narrative around behaviour, attendance and attainment, and their own passion for supporting square pegs and their families.

Over the last few years, changes in education have made it increasingly hard for those children who don't 'fit' the system – the square pegs.

Budget cuts, the loss of support staff, an overly academic curriculum, problems in the special educational needs and disabilities (SEND) system and difficulties accessing mental health support have all compounded pre-existing problems with behaviour and attendance. The 'attendance = attainment' and zero-tolerance narrative is often at odds with the way schools want to work with their communities, and many school leaders don't know which approach to take.

This book will be invaluable in guiding leaders and teaching staff through the most effective ways to address this challenge. It covers a broad spectrum of opportunity, from proven psychological approaches to technological innovations. It tests the boundaries of the current system in terms of curriculum, pedagogy and statutory Department for Education guidance. And it also presents a clear, legalese-free view of education, SEND and human rights law, where leaders have been given responsibility for its implementation but may not always fully understand the legal ramifications of their decisions or may be pressured into unlawful behaviour.

Suitable for all professionals working in education and the related issues surrounding children and young people's mental health, as well as policy-makers, academics and government ministers.

www.crownhouse.co.uk